Published by

www.povertyinitiative.org

poverty@uts.columbia.edu
3041 Broadway
New York, NY 10027
212-280-1439

Raising up generations of religious and community leaders committed to building a movement, led by the poor, to end poverty.

Appalachia: Listening With Our Hearts

Reflections on our immersion experience by students and faculty from Union Theological Seminary, students from Columbia University School of Social Work, and members of the Philadelphia Media Mobilizing Project

2007

Adam Barnes: article editing
Paul Chapman: article editing and copy editing
Katy Moore: copy editing and photo editing
Joe Strife: article editing and formatting
Alix Webb: copy editing
Colleen Wessel-McCoy: layout and design, formatting, article editing, and photo editing

Each of the following articles reflects the personal opinion of the author at the time it was written; we are still growing and learning.

Contents

Introduction

Paul Chapman and Liz Theoharis

In January 2007, the Poverty Initiative of the Union Theological Seminary offered a Field Education course for students from Union and the Columbia University School of Social Work. The course, called "Ending Poverty: An Immersion Experience in Appalachia," offered students an opportunity to explore issues of poverty and race in Appalachia and beyond, gain ideas and skills in organizing around issues of health care, housing, education, food and living wage jobs, and develop relationships with low-income leaders and members of the religious community.

It was the intention of this course to foster a sound Biblical and theological foundation for challenging the very existence of poverty in this wealthy land and for confronting global poverty in a world that has enough resources to feed, clothe and house everyone. We had made contact with some of the founders and members of organizations of poor people who were working to overcome the economic injustice of our society. It was our plan to meet with them, understand the challenges they face and the progress they are making, to build relationship and to learn from these leaders who are engaged in "the plight and the fight."

While many churches and social service agencies in the United States sponsor programs to alleviate the immediate pain of poverty, such as emergency food kitchens and shelters, we seek to find ways to eliminate poverty altogether, to render emergency food and shelter programs unnecessary. We believe that to do justice, poor people themselves, who are most affected by poverty, must take the lead in building a social movement with the goal of ending poverty. Throughout the course we were focused on hearing the voices of poor people themselves, listening to their stories and learning from them—gaining strength from their strength and identifying leaders whom we can support in their efforts to overcome the gross economic injustice that plagues America.

The trip

We gathered as a group for the first time at Union Theological Seminary in New York City for two days of orientation, including lectures, documentaries and group discussion, which we concluded with a visit to the city's largest men's shelter, located on Ward's Island, before climbing aboard a chartered bus that took us to Pittsburgh. From there, in rented vans, we traveled to Philippi, West Virginia, where we were hosted by Alderson-Broadus (A-B)

College. From this base we were able to divide into smaller groups to visit various communities and agencies in the area, as well as to attend lectures by AB faculty and community leaders to learn about socio-economic systems in Appalachia.

From Alderson-Broaddus, we traveled to Southeast Ohio where we were hosted by grassroots organizations connected with Organize! Ohio including Rural Action and the Appalachia People's Action Coalition. We returned to Charleston, West Virginia where leaders of Direct Action Welfare Group (DAWG), a statewide organization of poor families gathered religious and other community representatives to teach us about efforts to overcome poverty in West Virginia. Our trip concluded with a time of reflection at the Highlander Research and Education Center near Knoxville, Tennessee.

Who are we?

The instructors for the course were Willie Baptist, Scholar-in-Resident at Union, and Liz Theoharis, a Union Ph.D. candidate in Biblical studies. They were assisted by Dr. Jan Rehmann, a Union lecturer who traveled with us, as well as by Professors Brigitte Kahl and Barbara Lundblad who spoke to us during the orientation. The coordina-

Our travel caravan consisted of six rental minivans, two cars, and a luggage truck.
Parkersburg, WV
Photo: Colleen Wessel-McCoy

tor for the Immersion trip, who had spent six months preparing every detail, was Jessica Chadwick—a student at both Union and the Columbia University School of Social Work. She was assisted by Alix Webb, the Program Manager of the Poverty Initiative.

In addition to students from Union and Columbia, the trip included members of the Media Mobilizing Project in Philadelphia and several other friends of the Poverty Initiative.

The trip's participants came from many different faith traditions, from a diversity of racial, ethnic and cultural communities, from several nations, and from several sections of the United States and Canada. The youngest among us was born in 1984 and the oldest in 1931. Some of us were raised in economically comfortable circumstances and some of us grew up experiencing poverty first hand. Several participants continue to know poverty in their adulthood, understanding what it is like to have to choose between paying the rent and buying food. One thing we all have in common: the courageous leaders whom we met along the way were a source of inspiration as we each seek to find our way in a world of injustice.

Poverty in Appalachia and America

In his lecture that began our course orientation, Dr. Jan Rehmann underlined some of the myths that surround our understanding of poverty. It is widely assumed that poverty in the United States is primarily urban and black. Yet, the latest US Census reports that there are today a greater number of poor people living in non-urban areas than in cities; and there are more impoverished whites than blacks.

While a precise definition of poverty is difficult, the fact remains that millions of Americans are living in destitution—with inadequate food, housing, health care and educational opportunities. Millions who receive inadequate wages must struggle to survive. Credit card debt is out of control. Countless more are economically vulnerable—a pay check away from penury, threatened by eviction, mortgage foreclosures, bankruptcy and homelessness.

While throughout most of recorded history, there have been "haves" and "have-nots," in modern times there have also been decades of greater equalization. In the twenty years following the Second World War, the majority of Americans were enjoying increasing prosperity and the gap between rich and poor was narrowing. Yet, since the mid-1970s, statistics show that the economy has increasingly enriched the few at the expense of the many. We are well aware of the obscene incomes of CEO's of major corporations while the incomes of the workers stagnate, or their jobs are eliminated.

In writing about poverty in Appalachia, we realize that each individual's story is different and that generalizations tend to lump everyone together. During the course of our travels we met some of the individual people who are represented by the statistics, and have some insight into their valiant struggle to survive—their disappointments, their hopes, and their determination. We have learned from them, wept with them, laughed with them, sung with them, and prayed with them. They are our brothers and sisters—our friends.

We have also learned about the resilience and successful organizing efforts of many people in the Appalachian region. We met with community organizations, local congregations and ministries, social service providers and many others who are coming up with creative means of addressing and eliminating poverty. The history of struggle and community organizing is strong in Appalachia. We were emboldened by the passion and commitment of so many people we met.

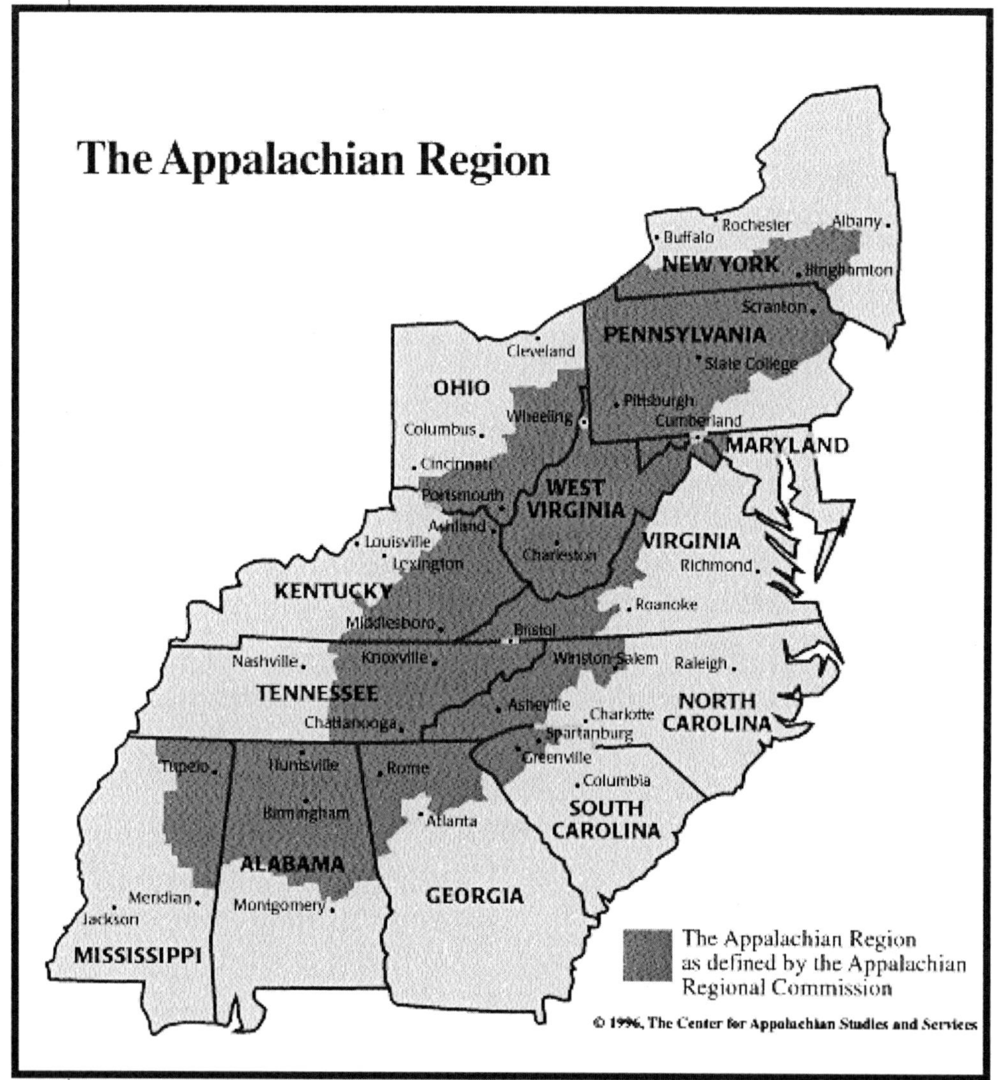

Poverty in Appalachia has many causes. For generations the natural resources of the area were the basis of the economy throughout much of Appalachia. But now the great stands of timber have been mostly cut and coal mining has changed so totally, as described in the following reflections, that far fewer employees now work in the mines, and the timber industry has all but disappeared.

Furthermore, the residents do not reap the profits of the rich veins of coal under their land. Seventy two percent of the surface area and eighty nine percent of the mineral rights are absentee-owned. Outsiders pay greatly reduced taxes—as little as $.25 per acre. In West Virginia, for example, a 1982 study showed that "absentee corporate landowners paid sixteen percent of the total state property tax, yet they owned fifty percent of the land and seventy-five percent of the mineral rights."

The loss of small and mid-sized manufacturing companies—companies that have moved abroad to profit from cheap labor—has also contributed to Appalachian unemployment, which runs as high as fifty percent in some counties. Retail jobs that pay close to minimum wages have not taken up the slack. Tourism that has helped rescue some rural areas of America has by-passed much of Appalachia. Isolation and the lack of good transportation makes access to health care, educational and cultural opportunities very difficult. Infrastructure improvements have not kept pace with the need.

The result of all this is serious economic deprivation. Thousands of families have no central plumbing, no telephones and no automobiles. We heard about communities that now have literally no economic base. Many young and working class people are forced to leave the area to find work, leaving the most vulnerable. Even as the economic situation deteriorates, federal funding programs have been cut back. The result is that the men, women and children of Appalachia have been left behind.

Yet, remarkably, many who have left Appalachia plan to return. The cultural magnetism of Appalachia is quite remarkable. The love of this land, the love of community, and family loyalty seem never to wane. We heard a number of people say that Appalachia is always their home, even while living in Chicago or elsewhere, and to home they will always return, even to be buried.

Susan Williams (left), Candie Carawan (center) and Guy Carawan (right), our hosts at the Highlander Center
New Market, TN
Photo: Colleen Wessel-McCoy

The unfair division of wealth in Appalachia is an unacceptable and unnecessary evil in our world. In a world of plenty, created by a God of love, poverty is blasphemy. While God loves all those that God has created, that love is demonstrated first and foremost in solidarity among the poorest and most marginalized. Despite efforts to sometimes blame poor people for their own condition, in Appalachia we witnessed strong and hard-working people who confront the daily grinding struggle of poverty with skills, insights and talents from which we can all learn.

Arts and culture

In appreciation of the talents and the rich cultural traditions of both Appalachia and past social movements, each night on our trip, we scheduled a cultural evening. We did a lot of singing, reflecting the musical heritage of the area. At the Highlander Research and Education Center, outside of Knoxville, where we spent our last days, we sang with Guy and Candie Carawan, professional musicians, who have long been associated with the vibrant musical tradition of Highlander. Songs from coal mining unions and songs from the Civil Rights era constituted our repertoire, but we also gained an appreciation that Appalachian music is a unique genre of folk music.

Our Biblical Mandate

Although the participants in this immersion course and contributors to this collection come from several different religious traditions and ethical frameworks, we gathered throughout our travel for biblical reflection. We focused on the book of Ruth in the Hebrew Scriptures. Historically, religion has played a unique and essential role in social movements. In the United States, Christianity has informed the abolitionist movement, women's suffrage movement and civil rights movement. Particularly for participants from Union Theological Seminary, as people of faith, we strive in our studies and in our lives to understand how God is acting in human history and how we can participate with God and one another in creating a world of justice and human fulfillment. In this endeavor we are guided and sustained by Sacred Scripture.

Throughout out trip we gathered for biblical reflection on the book of Ruth, led by Union student Erin Fleming (left).
Highlander Research and Education Center
New Market, TN
Photo: Colleen Wessel-McCoy

Key to our understanding of the Bible is the covenant between God and God's people. God has created and liberated the people from the bonds of exploitation in Egypt. God has cared for the people wandering in the wilderness by providing manna, just as much as people needed, and no more. And in covenant with the people, God requires loyalty to a life of justice and mercy. If one group accumulates more wealth than another, provision is made for the cancellation of debts and the redistribution of resources.

When, nevertheless, some people accumulated more than they needed and became rich, while others remained poor, the prophets cried out in the name of God. From a Biblical perspective, a people will be known by the situation of the most vulnerable in society, most often described as the widow, the orphan, the poor and the stranger.

The life of Jesus reflects these same values. In announcing his birth, Mary sings that the powerful will be brought down from their thrones and the lowly will be lifted up. The hungry have been filled and the rich sent empty away. (Luke 2:52-53) When Jesus begins his ministry, he says that God has anointed him to bring good news to the poor, and his life is lived among the poor and powerless. In his life and teaching, he defied and challenged the power of Imperial Rome, and for this he was executed. Those who seek to follow are called to live these same values—to clothe, to feed, to house, to visit... (Matthew 25)

The Poverty Initiative

In response to the crisis of poverty, domestically and internationally, the Poverty Initiative at Union Theological Seminary was founded to "raise up generations of religious and community leaders committed to building a movement, led by the poor, to end poverty." Poverty is a moral outrage, yet we have come to tolerate it in our midst. Sadly, America can rightly be described not as one nation, but as several, divided by wealth and poverty—the rich and powerful dominating the majority. How are we to serve as religious leaders and social workers in such a deeply divided world?

As the Poverty Initiative took root at Union in the fall of 2004, we invited a poor and formerly homeless man, Willie Baptist, who has dedicated his life to leadership education among poor people, to live amongst us at Union as a Scholar-in-Residence. With his counsel and following his example, we have sought to deepen the commitment of the Union community and the church to eliminate poverty, we have encouraged our faculty to include issues of poverty in their teaching and writing, and we have made connection with organized poor people from New York and around the country to invite them to Union to participate in classes, helping us deepen our understanding and resolve. In the spring of 2005 and again in the spring of 2007, we organized a Poverty Truth Commission, patterned on the projects in South Africa and Peru, in which poor people testified to both the realities of life in poverty in this rich land and their strategic struggles for justice. Leaders from the church, academia, media and the community served as Commissioners—listening, learning and deepening their own commitment to work for economic justice.

We are also deeply devoted to training other poor people to serve as Scholars-in-Residence in other seminaries and graduate schools throughout the country. This Poverty Scholars program has begun with a group of thirty five leaders from around the country, preparing to replicate and expand the program that began at Union. Already a number of seminaries and graduate schools have expressed an interest. Students at the Columbia University School of Social Work (CUSSW) have formed an active Poverty Initiative which cooperates closely with the Initiative at Union, and students from CUSSW were an important part of the Appalachia Immersion trip.

Already, the students in the Poverty Initiative are making plans for next year's Immersion Course. As we now envision the coming year, we will have more than one course, and we will invite anyone who is interested to share in this experience to join us. We plan to hold an Immersion Course to enable faculty, students and administrators who are interested in replicating the Poverty Initiative at their schools or religious institutions in how to organize immersion trips. Perhaps this group will return to Appalachia and another group from Union and beyond will visit the Mississippi Delta, another area where poverty is prevalent. The Delta was also the birth place of the Poor People's Campaign started by the Rev. Dr. Martin Luther King Jr. Two thousand and eight will be the 40th anniversary of this multi-racial campaign of poor people that started in Marks, Mississippi. We hope that you, the reader, will consider joining us on one of these immersion trips. We also would love to offer our consultation as your school or your congregation organizes your own mission or service-learning trip.

Appalachia immersion participants with Larry Gibson (in white jacket)
Kayford Mountain, WV
Photo: Sarah Smith, Media Mobilizing Project

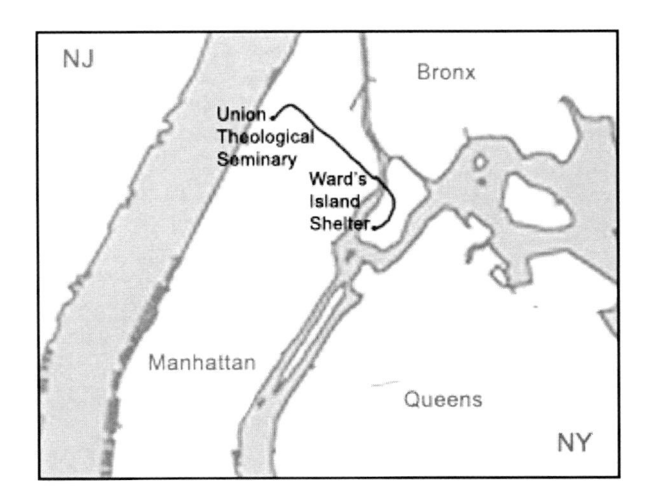

Orientation

Chapter 1

Itinerary:

Thursday, January 4, 2007

Gather at Union Theological Seminary, New York City, NY

Introduction to the issues and to the course

Lecture by Professor Barbara Lundblad on the importance of listening and the power of stories

Presentation by the Media Mobilizing Project: "Making Images: The Power and the Challenges"

Friday, January 5

Lecture by Dr. Jan Rehmann: "Poverty: What's Neoliberalism Got to Do With It?"

Lecture by Professor Brigitte Kahl: "Strategies of Resistance in the Book of Ruth"

Presentation by the Media Mobilizing Project: "Interviewing and Documentation Skills"

Presentation by William Burnett, Darren Gray and Owen Rogers of Picture the Homeless on Ward's Island Men's Shelter from the perspective of those who have stayed there

Travel to Ward's Island, New York to visit men's shelter, hosted by the Volunteers of America

Saturday, January 6

Travel from New York City to Philippi, West Virginia

Overnight at Alderson-Broaddus College

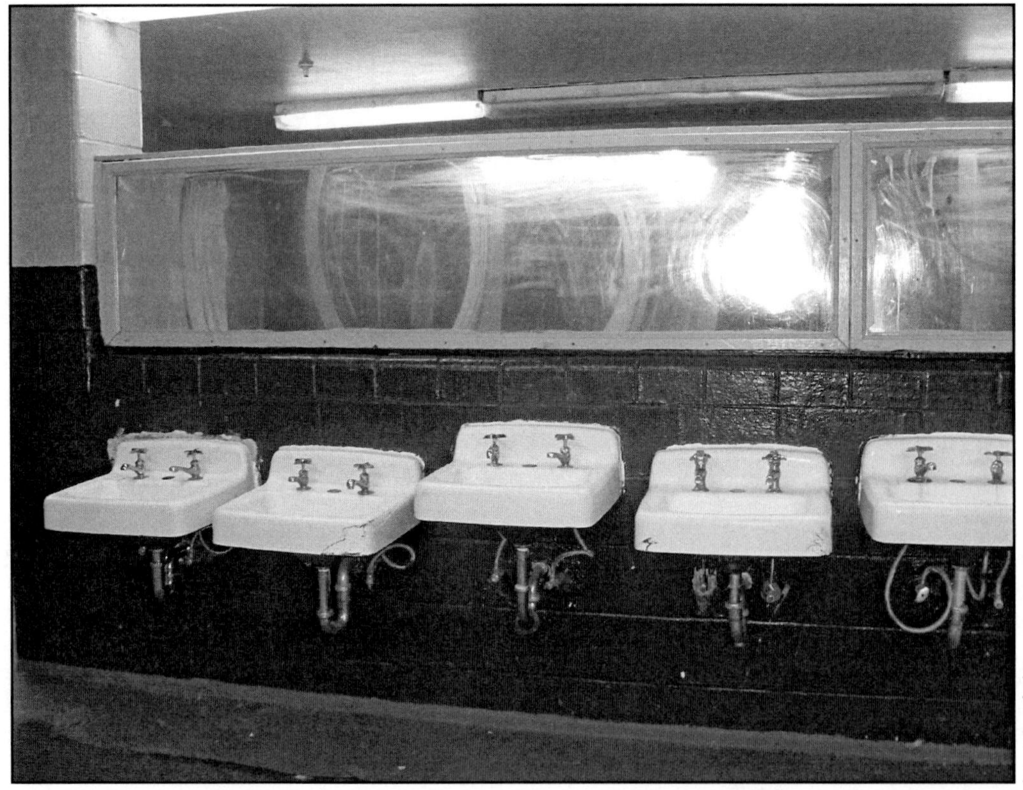

Men's shelter sinks
Wards Island, New York
Photo by Erica Almiron, Media Mobilizing Project

Willie Baptist and Brigitte Kahl
Union Theological Seminary, New York City
Photo: Paul Chapman

Men's shelter bathroom
Ward's Island, New York
Photo: Erica Almiron
Media Mobilizing Project

Paul Chapman
Poverty Initiative

With What Eyes Do I See?

During Saturday's orientation, we heard two sharply contrasting descriptions of a New York City men's shelter on Ward's Island. William Burnett, Darren Gray and Owen Rogers, three members of Picture the Homeless, described their life in the shelter—the rules, the regimentation, the foul smell, the chain link fence, the ubiquitous police, the strict regimentation, and the difficulty of getting to the shelter that requires a $4.00 bus ride, round trip. We were later given a guided tour of the same shelter by a gracious employee who showed us the facilities and described the caring work of the case workers, the recreation and art programs, the good food, the effort to find permanent housing and so forth.

Each of these people was speaking the truth and describing what they have experienced. So who shall we believe, since both sides have their truth? Presumably what we see in Appalachia will also depend upon our experience and our expectations. I expect to find the poverty by which Appalachia is known, but is this the poverty defined by the text books or by the people who live it? And what does poverty mean to them? Will I have the sensitivity to understand the situation through the eyes of those who live in Appalachia—who love the land, the music, the support of family and community and religion? Will I hear of their aspirations for better health care and education and infrastructure on their terms without imposing my own solutions?

The Nikki Giovanni poem that we read as a class, "Nikki-Rosa," likewise recognizes that one's situation influences the interpretation of what one sees and hears:

> I really hope no white person ever has cause to write about me
> because they never understand that love is Black wealth and they'll
> talk about my hard childhood and never understand that
> all the while I was quite happy.

For me the goal of this trip is to see from the perspective of those who are marginalized, those that the world sees last and counts least.

With a 953-bed capacity, the Charles H. Gay Center—the official name of the Ward's Island men's shelter—is the largest homeless shelter in New York City. It is run by Volunteers of America—one of the nation's oldest and largest faith-based human service organizations—founded in New York City in 1896. They offer services in over 200 cities, serve 1,800,000 people each year, and have an annual operating budget of $90 million.[1]

[1] Volunteers of America website: www.voa-gny.org/Content/Our_Programs-2035.asp and www.voa-gny.org/Content/About_Us-1004.asp. Submitted by Colleen Wessel-McCoy

Men's shelter showers without curtains
Wards Island, New York
Photo: Erica Almiron
Media Mobilizing Project

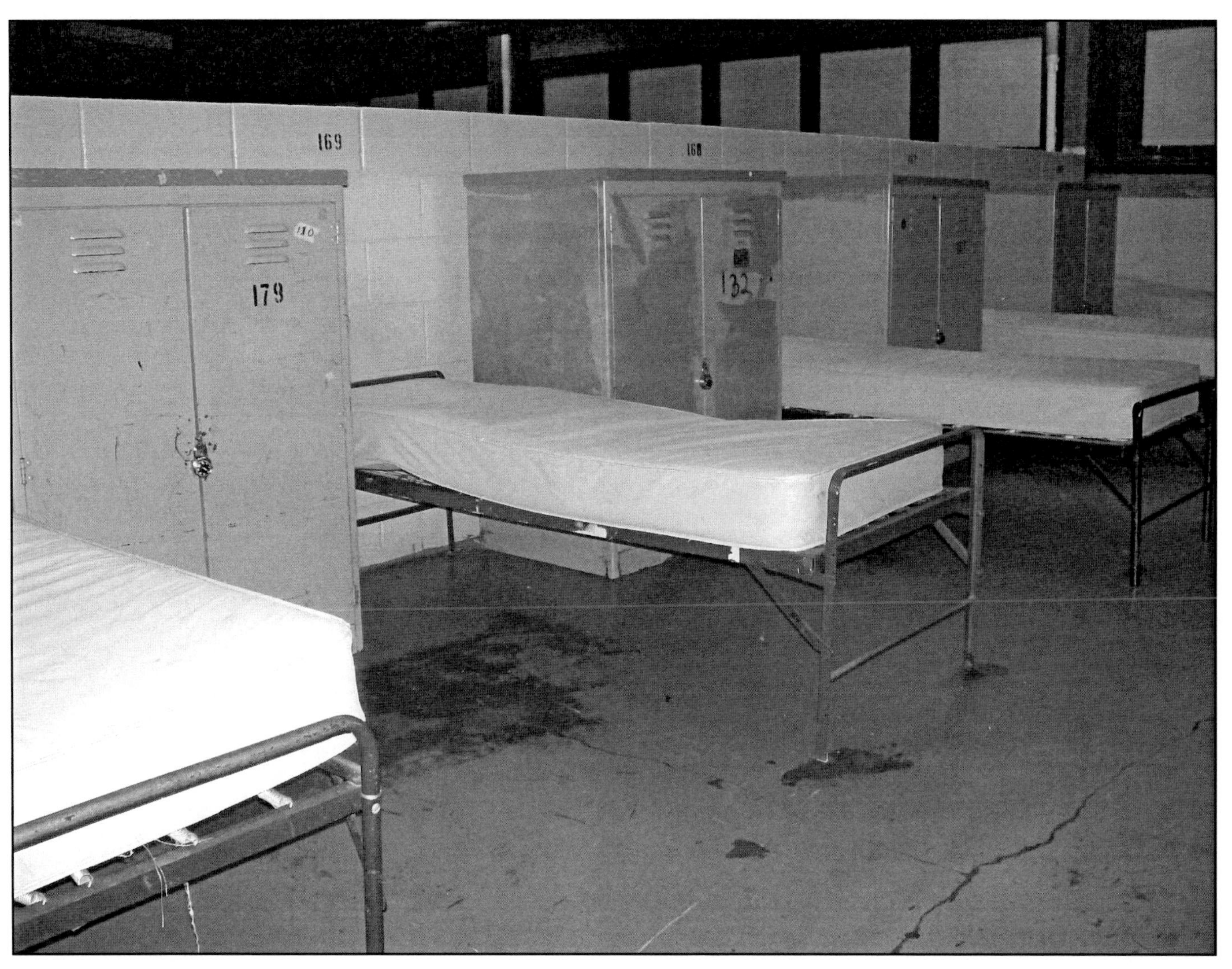

Men's shelter beds and lockers
Ward's Island, New York
Photo: Erica Almiron
Media Mobilizing Project

Union Theological Seminary
New York, NY
Photo: Erica Almiron
Media Mobilizing Project

Brigitte Kahl
Union Theological Seminary

Reading Ruth in Appalachia

Two women are on the road. Where they come from is a home that no longer exists—dreams and hopes they had to bury, together with the three men who died, a family that ceased to exist. A series of tragic events has swept them to the bottom of society, impoverished, without security and without belonging anywhere. They had to leave. Rumors are in the air about a place called "House of Bread", Beth-lehem, where God granted food after a long period of hunger. But will there be bread for them in the city of bread? They don't really belong there either—Ruth from Moab, the country of Israel's archenemies, and Naomi, her mother-in-law who had left Bethlehem during the famine many years ago. At that time they were desperate to make a living elsewhere, even in Moab. And Naomi still had a husband and two sons. Now she is all by herself, hapless and empty, a migrant elderly widow returning from whence she came, together with her young Moabite daughter-in-law.

They are an odd couple, the two of them. Chances are that there will also be no bread for them in Bethlehem, the house of bread. What makes them believe that they have even a right to ask? The field Naomi's husband once owned is long gone, and without a son she has no legal means to reclaim it. Naomi's time is over and maybe she just wants go back to her native soil to die. She had told Ruth and her other daughter-in-law that they surely had better chances to survive anywhere else than in Bethlehem and with someone called Naomi, the barren, bitter and cursed one. This is no longer the time for loving-kindness, affection, clinging together. Facing the brutal realities of life, everyone has to look after herself. Why did Ruth not listen? Why did she come at all?

So far, this is a story written and re-written in millions of variations all over the world until today, in the big and small movements of humanity throughout history in search of bread and a better life. Or simply survival. Why is it a story worth reading on a trip to Appalachia in January 2007? And what precisely makes it a Biblical story? You will have to find an answer for yourself. The people in Appalachia are not exactly immigrants. But like Ruth and Naomi many of them are women exposed to poverty in very specific ways. Together with their communities they are engaged in the precarious struggles of those "not entitled" to get their share from the bread-houses of the country. And from the rich natural resources of the land that is, and is not, theirs. The poor needn't be newcomers or foreigners in a technical sense to stay excluded from the distribution of social wealth; they are made strangers and refugees no matter where they were born.

As it happens, they often cannot afford the luxury of leading lives that never cross the boundaries of the established morality and order. Those who had a secure home and three meals a day in Bethlehem wouldn't need to go to the threshing floor in the middle of the night like Ruth, to seduce a man much older than she, but with power over grain and hearth. Naomi, Ruth, and Boaz all take great care that the "transgression" doesn't come to light. Because all of a sudden somebody in the village might feel that Ruth threatens the wellbeing of the community—an illicit immigrant, alien by nature and intolerable in her behavior. Somebody actually could play the "Moabite card"—aren't the Moabites known for sexual perversions of all kinds that probably go back to Sodom where they all come from? (Gen 18-19) The poor are never safe. Ruth has risked a lot.

Maybe at this point we touch something that is at the very core of Ruth's story as a Biblical story: righteousness in the eyes of God is something other than law and order. It can be right there in the murkiness and messiness of survival strategies where the poor have no choice, and in all the grey zones of illegal existence where the self-declared advocates of moral values see immorality all over the place. Like her much older ancestress Tamar in the book of Genesis (Gen 38), Ruth may be condemned by the law of self-righteousness. But she is justified through God—and through the mercy and unfaltering loyalty she embodies for another needy person who is cut off from life and land like herself: Naomi, the bitter one.

The narrative of Ruth was probably written in the 4th century B.C.E. after Israel's return from the Babylonian exile when questions of social ordering and re-organization were an issue, e.g. with regard to "mixed marriages" with foreigners. The story itself, however, is set approximately six centuries further back in the pre-monarchic time of the Judges when Israel lived in a sedentary society where kinship and family and the land are the basic networks that enable an individual to survive. Neither king nor any state apparatus is in place; rather Torah, the law of God is supposed to guide the life of the people. The council of the elders decides matters of importance for the community. In a way, God could be seen as king and supreme ruler. At the very beginning of the story, Naomi's husband is introduced by the name of Elimelech, which means "my God is king." The question raised all throughout Ruth thus would be: what does it mean if the law of God guides a society, and more specifically, how does such a "kingdom of God" deal with hunger and with the poor inside and outside its boundaries? Who has a right to claim the land, dig into its mountains, harvest its wealth? And by what rules are the bread houses of a society kept open or shut for those without food?

Boaz, the kinsman of Naomi, illustrates the case to be made. He emerges as a truly righteous man who operates from the inside but tries to make the legal system work for those outside the law and beyond anybody's responsibility. At the gate of the city, where the council of elders meets, he turns and pushes and squeezes the letter of the law until it says what he knows it means—that the poor widow has a right to reclaim her land and a place to live. It has been often observed that the legal construct of the "redeemer"—the one who according to biblical law is obliged to restore land, freedom and family endurance to a close relative who has lost any of it—functions in a quite unusual way in the book of Ruth. But it seems that for Boaz this is just the right way to be law-abiding: to help out those who fall through the cracks of the law. Because at the core of the Bible, law is not a blind Lady Justice with her eyes covered, but a justice that sees through the eyes of mercy.

The mercy that Ruth had shown to Naomi and her family when they were foreigners in Moab (Ruth 1:8), and then later when she herself is a foreigner in Bethlehem, was far above any legal obligation of the Moabites. Righteous-ness–with–mercy is what Boaz practices both towards Ruth, the stranger, and Naomi, the estranged. Since God heard the cries of Hebrew aliens pressed into slave labor and below–subsistence–level conditions under Pharaoh's rule (Exodus 3), this merciful righteousness stands against the murderous imperial law of Egypt, in whatever country "Egypt" might take over—even in the land of Israel itself. The book of Ruth only rarely talks about God explicitly, but by raising the very question of what justice and law might mean in the case of the "non-deserving" widow, the foreigner, the poor, it talks about nothing less than who we believe God really is (Ruth 2:11f). The poor are the test-case that may help us know whether the faith of God's people is really still faith in God, or whether it has meanwhile quietly mutated into imperial worship and idolatry.

But a Moabite? Why of all people must Ruth be from Moab? In Appalachia, one comes across "hillbillies" and "rednecks" and "poor white trash" alongside black poverty—here arises the perpetual question of images of the "other" that we carry with us no matter how much they damage our own cause. Moabites in the Old Testament are a good example of stereotyping and "othering" among non-hegemonic groups. The story that sticks to them ineradicably is how their ancestress, desperate to have a child, drugged and seduced her father Lot in the middle of the night, not long after they all had escaped the disaster of Sodom and Gomorrah (Genesis 19). Moabites are often portrayed as enemies of God's people, somebody to stay away from and not to mix with. They are seen as having transgressed religiously and morally. When Naomi sends Ruth to Boaz in the middle of the night, does she expect her to do what a Moabite does? It never becomes entirely clear all throughout the book the extent to which Naomi is able to leave her own anti-Moabite prejudices behind and to treat Ruth as her equal. But when Ruth, through Boaz, becomes the mother of a new son to Naomi, the female neighbors declare that Ruth the Moabite is more precious to Naomi than seven sons (Ruth 4:14f). In the patriarchal world of the story, this is a very remarkable statement.

In the end, it is the solidarity between the two women that makes them survive against all odds. Neither of them could have done it by herself. There were enough cultural and social barriers that could have left them as enemies and rivals, or at least oblivious and indifferent to each other's plight. All too often we have seen how those who are tied together through poverty and social degradation, and who would desperately need one another to make a difference, are torn apart along racial, social, cultural and religious rifts or even simply split along personal lines of mutual contempt. In the book of Ruth, the choice is either staying together or perishing. Neither the strength, nor the despair, of an isolated Self, but the outreaching compassion and companionship of the Other turns death into life. From the perspective of Israelite pride and self-esteem, it is a stark challenge that all depends on a Moabite. Ruth's oath of allegiance to her mother-in-law (Ruth 1:16f)—the text that today, ironically, has become a standard inventory of heterosexual marriage ceremonies—turns not only the "law" of the patriarchal household order upside-down, but also disrupts the self-centered law of any society obsessed with power (as hierarchy and competition) that can even make the poor fight against each other rather than against poverty. Powerless as they are, Ruth and Naomi empower each other, when Naomi had thought nothing was left for her other than a solitary death. In the Bible, these two women teach one of the most significant lessons of solidarity, the lesson that it is not "power-over" but "power-with" that is able to create new life out of the nothingness of nobodies: a child born to the barren, bitter, and empty one.

Seen from this angle, the book of Ruth is much more than an individual story of two women happily ending up in a man's house again. It is a social and theological parable impregnated with a profoundly transformative vision, much like the songs sung by Hannah in 1 Samuel 2 and by Mary and Elizabeth in Luke 1. With Obed, the son of Ruth, Naomi, and Boaz, the great-grandfather of King David is born, a decisive ancestor of Jesus Christ according to Matthew's gospel (Matthew 1:5). Obed is the "Other" that is physically and forever implanted into the body of Israel and the body of Christ. Obed represents the presence of the poor, the widow, and the stranger in our midst as a persistent challenge and opportunity for the kingdom of David and any subsequent political order: the challenge and opportunity to change towards justice. Obed is the living memory both in Israel and in the church that the land belongs to God and therefore needs to be treated respectfully, that land and life have to be restored for those who have lost it—and that poverty is a litmus test not only for the social order but also for theology. For whenever the poor are let back into society, God is let back.

Reading the book of Ruth in Appalachia and throughout this journey you will see things you never would learn in a classroom. It will question many images of poverty and of God that we take for granted much more than we are aware of, including the image of poverty as a "given" that is inescapably built into the world order since God created it. Meaning-making is closely related to context, seeing and blindness to social location, even physical location. Go and see how the book of Ruth reads on the road, and how the land and the poor of Appalachia, as conversation partners, will change your reading.

Jan Rehmann
Union Theological Seminary

Poverty—What's Neoliberalism Got to Do With It?

Common Sense and Social Analysis

"In my neighborhood, I've seen a welfare recipient driving a BMW—there is so much fraud going on," one of my students at the City University of New York said in a class discussion, and it was evident that this story considerably framed how she perceived welfare recipients. I later learned that she grew up in poverty herself and as a single mother still struggled to make ends meet. This was, for her, the dignified poverty, the acceptable one that has nothing to do with welfare, the virtuous one where you work hard and pull yourself up by your bootstraps. It was not that she was insensitive towards the problem; there is no need to tell her how poverty felt. But it remained a purely individual issue, to be resolved in private. Her world view was structured by the dichotomy of "deserving" and "undeserving" poor.

I am telling you this story because it reveals the weight of common sense on our perception and understanding of the world around us, demonstrating the importance of a critical social analysis. According to Antonio Gramsci's famous definition, common sense is an incoherent set of generally held assumptions and beliefs. "It contains Stone Age elements and principles of a more advanced science, prejudices from all past phases of history [...] and intuitions of a future philosophy," and the task of a "philosophy of praxis" is then to critically work on the coherence of common sense.[1] Each ideology that tries to build up political consent has to anchor itself in common sense by connecting with certain of its elements splitting them from or pitting them against others. When we are confronted with poverty, we usually have certain images and explanations that we think are authentic, coming out of what we've seen and experienced directly. In fact, these preconceptions are often determined by the prevailing media images and the predominant ideologies about poverty.

---

[1] Antonio Gramsci, *Selections from the Prison Notebooks of Antonio Gramsci,* edited by Quintin Hoare and Geoffrey Nowell Smith, International Publisher: New York, 1971, pp. 324, 330-31.

A widespread common-sense understanding is that poverty is due to individual fate or bad choices people make in their lives: dropping out of college, getting pregnant, getting divorced, ending up in one of the famous female-headed families that haunt the "moral" debates on poverty, having a "culture of poverty," sliding into the "black underclass" of the inner-city ghettos, lacking an education, failing to adapt to the demands of the economy, etc. And some of us might know examples where certain fateful events, choices or cultural characteristics actually do play a role. We might even know welfare recipients (or have heard about them) who are "lazy," drug addicted, or who cheat the system—examples that seem to validate the impression that these characteristics are the causes of poverty.

Social analysis can help us to mistrust such widespread images. This might start on the basic level of statistics that contradict the widespread myth of the "lazy" poor: in 1997, 48% of poor families with children had at least one family member that worked full time, 29% had at least one family member that worked part time, while only 24% were excluded from the labor market.[2] If you add up the full time and part time percentages, you can see that over three quarters were indeed "connected" to the labor market, and less than a quarter were not. Poverty is therefore not sufficiently understood as people being "excluded" from the labor market and its beneficial "work ethics" for "psychological" or "cultural" reasons. It is more accurately described as the destiny of working poor who actually work their hearts out, while exploitation or the lack of sustainable jobs prevents them from getting out of poverty.

One of the differences between common-sense notions and social analysis is the latter's insistence on carefully distinguishing between structural causes of poverty as a mass phenomenon and the psychological and cultural consequences, i.e. the ways poverty is being lived and experienced. For example, no one would deny that alcohol and drug abuse play a devastating role in poor communities—nobody knows this better than poor people's movements whose organizing efforts are constantly undermined by drug trafficking and addiction. But it does not make sense when one tries to explain the mass impoverishment in the de-industrialized "Rust Belt" or in the devastated coal mining areas of Appalachia by blaming the drug trade or specific cultural patterns. Even if it might sound simplistic, the statement "It's the economy, stupid, does more to explain the reality than highly sophisticated deliberations about the "culture of poverty."

And finally, social analysis can help to reconstruct how the images of poverty that we've got in our heads have been carefully prepared by think tanks, produced by the media and other ideological apparatuses. It can enable us to critically challenge what presents itself as spontaneous evidence. One example is the racialization of the image of poverty that started in the mid-60s: before 1964, the predominant media representation of poverty was the

---

[2] According to the National Academy of Sciences poverty measure. Cf. John Iceland, *Poverty in America. A Handbook.* Second Edition, University of California Press: Berkeley, Los Angeles, London, 2006, pp. 78-79.

white rural poor of the Appalachian coalfields. These pictures of the "good poor," the "deserving poor," stirred up the public sympathy and helped support President Johnson's "War on Poverty." But by 1967, 72% of media representations of the poor were African-Americans, and the "undeserving poor" have become mostly black.[3] Poverty was increasingly identified with a black ghetto "underclass," a dangerous outsider phenomenon, cut off from our booming economy and disconnected from the American dream and its moral values. These images enforced racist reactions among the white middle class and blue collar workers who saw their tax money being wasted for inner-city hustlers and drug addicts. The ideological connection of poverty and black crime prepared the ground for turning the "war against poverty" into a "war against the poor."

The widespread explanations of poverty by psychological or cultural factors suffer from the fundamental weakness that they dissimulate the social structures by which poverty is being produced, the relations of power in our economy, the way the riches in this rich country are being distributed. I'd like to focus on the connection between poverty and the system of social inequality, and for this purpose I'll go back a bit in history to the late 1970s and early 1980s, because it is at that time that the market radicalism that we experience today came to power.

Increasing Social Injustice

Data from *The State of Working America* (2006-2007) helps illuminate this shift. Figure 1 shows the income share of the top 10% of the population from 1913 to 2003, comparing the US and France. Generally speaking, it shows that the richest 10% proportionately accumulated a much larger portion of the pie. If we look at the time span between 1953 and 1973, we can see that this top bracket of the US population owned little more than 30%, whereas the French upper classes were relatively better off, owning up to over 35% in the 1960s. But the dynamics changed at the end of the 1970s and beginning of the 1980s: the top-decile share of income in the US reached 44% in 2000, while the share of the French elites remained relatively low.

A similar tendency can be seen in Figure 2, which compares the family income of the top 0.1% of the population of three countries (US, UK, France). We can see again that between the 1950s and the mid-1970s their share remains quite stable (between 2 and 3% of the national income). And then, the US share rocketed upwards in the late 1970s and early 1980s (reaching about 7.4% in 1998), leaving the elites of the other two countries far behind. The two charts illustrate how the income inequality has increased in the last thirty years, especially in the US. The ratio of the median compensation of a worker to the median salaries of a CEO was still 1:30 in 1970, but by 2000 the ratio had soared to 1:500.[4]

---

[3] Cf. Martin Gilens, "How the Poor Became Black. The Racialization of American Poverty in the Mass Media," in: Schram, Sanford F., Joe Soss, and Richard C. Fording (ed.), *Race and the Politics of Welfare Reform*, The University of Michigan Press: Ann Arbor, 2003, pp. 101-130.

[4] Cf. David Harvey, *A Brief History of Neoliberalism*, Oxford University Press: Oxford, 2005, p. 16.

Figure 1 Top decile income share in France and in the United States

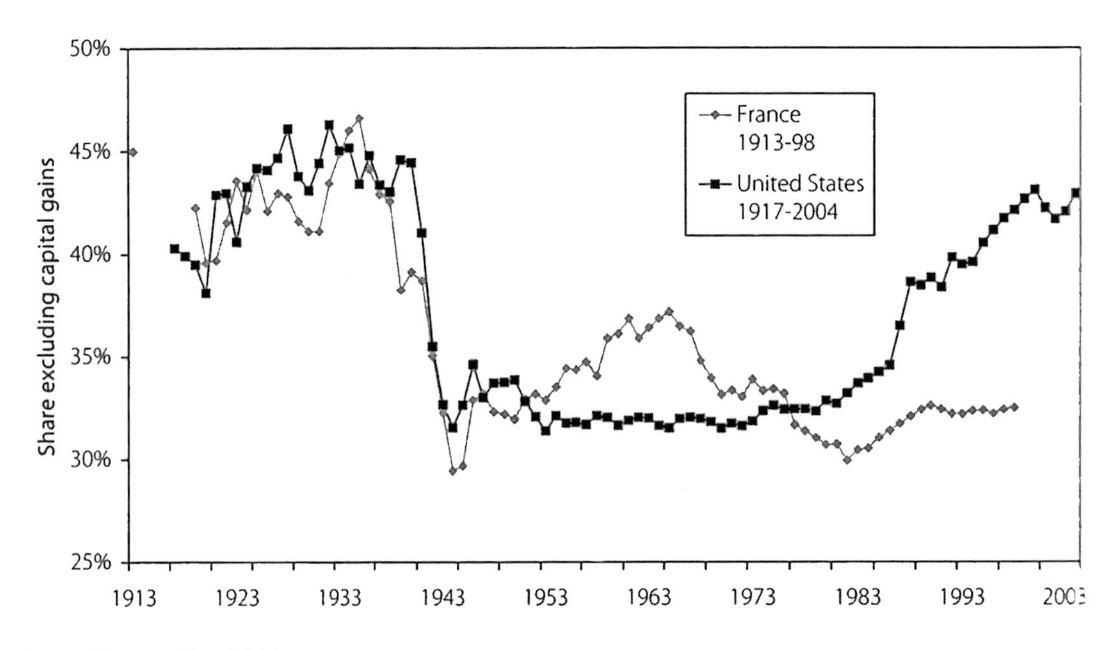

Source: Piketty and Saez (2001).

Figure 2 Top 0.1% family income share in France, the United States, and the United Kingdom

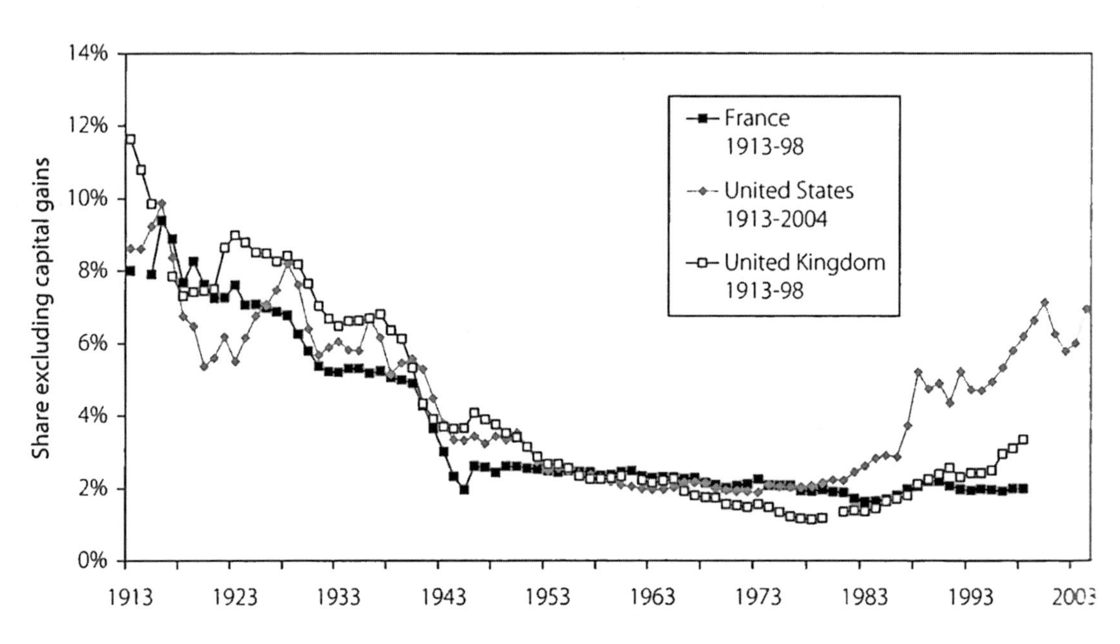

Source: Piketty and Saez (2001).

What happened in between? Why did the income inequality increase so sharply from the late 1970s onwards? One of the answers points to the predominance of "neoliberalism" that begins at that time.

A Neoliberal Theology of the Market

What is neoliberalism? The term is not to be confused with the common use of "liberal" in the US, which usually designates a moderate left wing attitude, concerned with the welfare state, social justice, and tolerance. Neoliberalism is rather the opposite. It has become the general designation for an ideology and politics centered on the functioning of a capitalistic market that is "free" from government interference, especially from any attempt of wealth redistribution in favor of lower classes or marginalized groups. Its proponents advocate the dismantling of the welfare state, deregulation of labor relations, and the weakening of trade unions' bargaining power, all in the name of a "free market society" and its entrepreneurial spirit, both of which are in danger of being stifled by a patronizing state bureaucracy. Proclaiming "individual freedom," neoliberalism proposes to bring all human actions and desires into the domain of the market, since it considers market exchange as an "ethic in itself," capable of substituting for all previously held ethical beliefs.[5]

Contrary to the polemics against government interference that are often part of neoliberal rhetoric, neoliberalism's economic politics were first implemented around 1975 by Pinochet's cruel dictatorship in Chile—with the active support of the "Chicago School" around Milton Friedman. But neoliberalism's hegemony cannot be reduced to force or forgery. It has become an ideology with a strong impact on common sense, an ideology that could win an active or at least passive consensus, not only among elites, but also among wider milieus of middle and popular classes. In the US it has taken on a kind of religious aura that permeates everyday culture to a degree we are often not aware. Its victory became clear with the election of Margret Thatcher in 1979 in the UK and of Ronald Reagan in 1980 in the US.

Looking to the origins of neoliberal theory, I confine this discussion to one of its leading figures, Friedrich Hayek, an Austrian economist and philosopher, who emigrated from Austria to London in 1931, and then, in 1950, to Chicago. In 1947, he organized the first international association, the Mont Pèlerin Society, that helped spread many neoliberal think tanks all over the world. His *Road to Serfdom* (1944) became a bible for the British neoliberals around Margret Thatcher. In 1976, he published *The Mirage of Social Justice*, in which he demonstrated that the concept of social justice, in any form, is empty and misleading.[6] Employing the term is either thoughtless or fraudulent, a dishonest insinuation that is intellectually disreputable and destructive of moral feeling. Why?

---

[5] Cf. David Harvey, *A Brief History of Neoliberalism*, Oxford University Press: Oxford, 2005, p. 3.

[6] Hayek, Friedrich A., *Law, Legislation and Liberty, Vol 2: The Mirage of Social Justice*, University of Chicago Press: Chicago and London, 1976, pp. XII, 97.

Justice can only exist among individuals, he assumes, and therefore cannot be applied to the "Great Society of free men," which he defines as (and actually reduces to) the anonymous and spontaneous mechanisms of the market. He frankly admits this market "gives to those who already have. But this is its merit rather than its defect."[7] One cannot apply a standard of "social justice" if there is no one in charge who can be blamed and to whom one could appeal if the standard is not met. The market is like a "game" with its own rules, and when you lose you have to accept the outcome as fate.

If we step back and look at Hayek's arrangement, we can see that he establishes the market as a kind of deity whose decrees are to be followed without questioning and whose realm is not to be touched by human planning or reasoning. Its invisible hand has some interesting functional similarities to the deeds of a hidden God, *deus absconditus*, in Calvinist theology: it cannot be known. For Hayek, the claim to understand the spontaneous workings of the market constitutes a fundamental fallacy of the Age of Reason, which he associates most notably with the traditions of Marx and Freud. It cannot and must not be influenced. Any attempt to interfere in the market game in the sense of redistributive justice leads straight to full-fledged socialism and is totalitarian by definition.[8] But while Hayek's portrayal of the market is reminiscent of the ideological form of traditional theology, it is also the exact opposite of its Judaic-Christian substance. Hayek's hidden God is definitely not the biblical God of the Exodus and the Jubilee Year, of liberation and social justice, but the reified rule of money, capital, and shareholder values, i.e. the very fetishism the Bible so forcefully condemns as idolatry, epitomized by the golden calf.

As Fredric Jameson remarks, the neoliberals' free market is Leviathan in sheep's clothing.[9] Market totalitarianism is indeed incompatible with a Christian ethics that starts from the sacredness of the human person, "realized in community with others," because from this ethical perspective the economic institutions have to "serve" human needs, and not the other way around. In the words of a famous 1986 Catholic Pastoral Letter: "Wherever our economic arrangements fail to conform to the demands of human dignity lived in community, they must be questioned and transformed."[10] From Hayek's starting point of an unquestionable market game, it is consistent that he turns against any notion of economic human rights. In his view, President Roosevelt's Four Freedoms (of speech, of worship, from want, from fear) and the United Nations' Universal Declaration of Human Rights (that proclaims the social right to decent jobs, housing, health care and education) are fundamentally flawed because they combine individual freedoms with social and economic rights, which he says are not compatible with a market society

---

[7] ibid., 123.

[8] ibid. 64, 75-6, 136.

[9] F. Jameson, *Postmodernism, or, The Cultural Logic of Late Capitalism*, Duke University Press: Durham, 1991, p. 273.

[10] *Economic Justice for All. Pastoral Letter on Catholic Social Teaching and the US Economy*, 1986, p. 15.

and lead to socialism.[11] But the totalitarian state socialism he invokes is more part of a scarecrow scenario than the real target, which is the "social-liberal" attempt to connect individual and social rights. Neoliberalism first and foremost targets the economic doctrine of Keynesianism and the social compromise it represented.

The Dismantling of the Keynesian Welfare State

Keynesianism was the mainstream economic doctrine in the US and Western Europe between WWII and the late 1970s. The term is derived from the economist John Maynard Keynes (1883-1946), counselor of the British government, who advocated the very economic politics Hayek, Milton Friedman and other neoliberals strictly rejected: a mixed economy, in which both the state and the private sector play an important role; an active fiscal policy oriented toward the macroeconomic goals of economic growth, full employment, and citizens' welfare. Such goals are all excluded from Hayek's concept of a purposeless society; most notably, Keynes advocated the state's responsibility to strengthen the demand side, e.g. raising real wages, so that people have enough money to buy the commodities businesses produce. Keynes, whose doctrine had a strong impact on Roosevelt's New Deal politics, was certainly not a "socialist." When he stepped into the debates about how to overcome the Economic World Crisis, he promised not to institute revolution but to save capitalism. "He was pro-business and pro-entrepreneur, but was very critical of *rentiers* and speculators," summarizes Wikepedia.[12] According to his economic doctrine, the government has the responsibility to pursue macroeconomic policies that ensure people have long lasting jobs, decent wages, and social protection systems. In other words, it has the duty to provide some social justice by re-distributing the wealth towards the lower-income segments.

For a long time, neoliberalism was a minority movement of intellectuals that could not match the predominance of Keynesianism in public opinion. But this began to change in the 1970s when the economy stagnated and the economic and political elites came to the conviction that Keynesian strategies did not work anymore. The changing tide could be seen in 1974 and 1976, when Friedrich Hayek and then Milton Friedman received the Nobel Prize in economics. Four years later, Margret Thatcher and Ronald Reagan were in power.

Looking back at the increase of social inequality from the early 1980s onward, illustrated by figures 1 and 2, we can see what was really going on behind the smokescreen of anti-government and market "freedom" slogans. Neoliberalism in practice can be described as the successful strategy of the elites to restore their economic power as well as political and ideological hegemony. The neoliberals achieved this goal by different means, out of which I only select a few:

[11] ibid. 103-04.

[12] Wikepedia, "Keynesian economics."

- In terms of financial markets, the beginning of neoliberalism can be described as the transition from the "Bretton Woods System" to a new "Dollar-Wall Street-Regime" in the early 1970s. By abolishing gold as the material anchor of money flows ("Nixon shock") and by abandoning the fixed currency prices among nation states, most of the international financial relations were taken out of the control of state central banks and turned over to private financial operators.[13] The economic balance of power shifted to private banks and created the predominance of a financial sector over the productive sector—a specific "disembedded" variety of capitalism, frequently dubbed "turbo-capitalism" (Edward Luttwak) or "casino capitalism" (Susan Strange).

- The Reagan administration and its successors issued dramatic tax cuts for the rich, in both corporate taxes and top personal tax rates. As you can see in Figure 3, between 1979 and 1990 the tax rate for the highest bracket dropped from 70% to 28%.

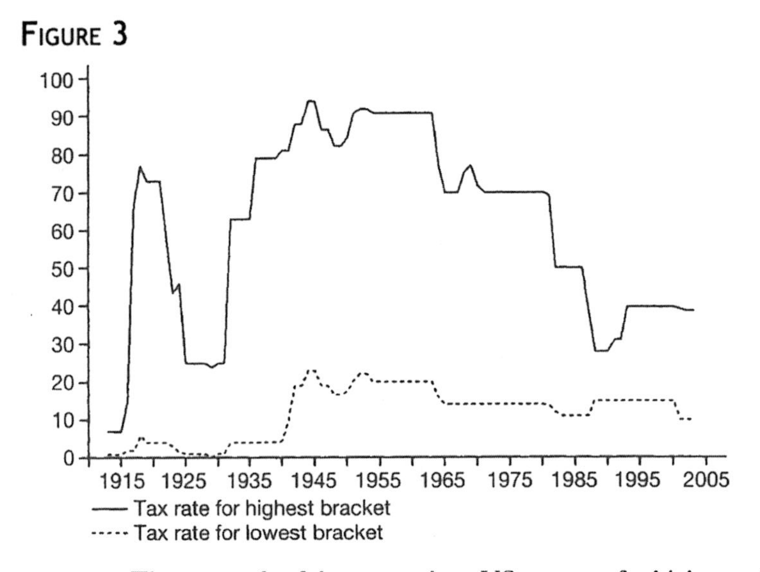

The tax revolt of the upper class: US tax rates for higher and lower brackets, 1913–2003

Source: Duménil and Lévy, 'Neoliberal Income Trends'.

- Reagan's victory over the air traffic controllers' union (PATCO) marked the beginning of a massive assault on labor unions. Figure 4 shows that the proportion of unionized workers declined from 29% in 1975 to

---

[13] Cf. Peter Gowan, *The Global Gamble. Washington's Faustian Bid for World Dominance*, Verso: London, New York, 1999, pp. 17-30.

12.5% in 2005. At the same time, capital investments moved away from the unionized northeast and midwest into the non-union south and west. This decline had an immediate effect on poverty, regardless of what one thinks about the quality and political integrity of labor unions. Often, the mere existence of a union makes the difference between working in poverty and working your way out of poverty.

Figure 4 **Union coverage rate in the United States, 1977-2005***

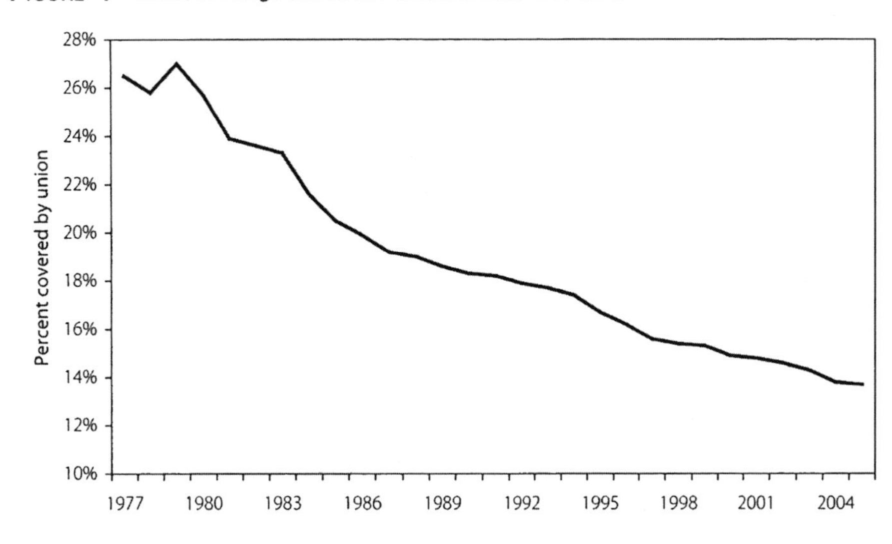

* Covered by a collective bargaining agreement.
Source: Hirsch and Macpherson (1997) and BLS.

- The economy was deregulated; the government withdrew, and public services like transportation, education, the care for the environment, the supply of energy and water were increasingly privatized and commodified. In terms of labor relations, deregulation means basically that employers can hire and fire their workforce as they like. It is one of neoliberalism's main characteristics that engendered a considerable increase of unsecured, contingent labor, especially for women.

- An overall tendency is the "Wal-Martization" of the economy. Wal-Mart is not only the world's largest corporation, but it also models a new type of low-salary and low-benefit employment practice that systematically bulldozes small business in the neighborhood by dropping prices. Wal-Mart's salaries are often not enough to lift a family above the poverty level; its health care packages are so expensive that over half of its employees cannot afford them and are therefore forced to rely on Medicaid and other government programs financed by taxes. All of a sudden, the much-vilified role of the state in the economy becomes vital again, but only as a source of corporate subsidies: taxpayers have to absorb the health care costs for the employees of a corporation with huge annual profits.

This is a very incomplete list of how Neoliberalism has worked in practice. One of its outcomes can be observed in Figure 5, which shows wage decline starting again at the end of the 1970s, interrupted by a rise from 1995 to 2000 in the famous "New Economy" period, but ended by the recession of 2001. The most remarkable finding in this chart lies in the relationship between wage levels and the productivity curve. From the 1960s to the mid

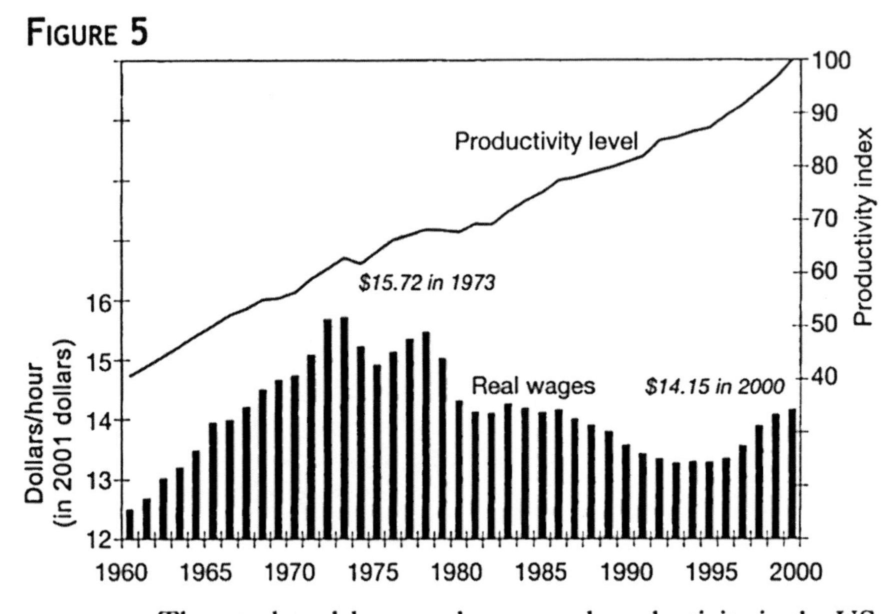

The attack on labour: real wages and productivity in the US, 1960–2000

Source: Pollin, *Contours of Descent*.

1970s, you can see a correlation between the increase of productivity and the increase of wages—which corresponds to a basic common-sense notion of "fairness": when the pie gets bigger, the salaries should go up as well. But from the late 1970s onwards, this correlation is broken up. Although productivity rates accelerated again from 2000 to 2005,[14] real wages fell and the number of families in poverty grew.

From the "War on Poverty" to the "War against the Poor"

The hegemony of Neoliberalism had its immediate consequences in the general perception of welfare politics and poverty. This was shown in the prevailing opinion (famously laid out in Murray's *Losing Ground*) that poverty

[14] Cf. *The State of Working America 2006/2007*, ed. by Lawrence Mishel, Jared Bernstein, Sylvia Allegretto, Cornell University Press: Ithaca, 2007, pp. 17-21.

was mainly caused by the welfare programs themselves. The argument is simple: It's not the social structure or the class position that determines your economic success but rather the individual choices you make. The social welfare programs established by Roosevelt's New Deal and augmented by Johnson's War on Poverty created negative incentives that keep people in poverty—not taking a poorly paid job, not staying in school, not getting married—because this would reduce the welfare benefits. In this explanation we see "welfare queens" collecting their money from different agencies. The moral decline constitutes an irresponsible and criminal "culture of poverty," the culture of a "ghetto underclass" that perpetuates poverty. The argument is based on the (counterfactual) assumption that the poor could work themselves out of poverty if they just tried hard enough.

This pattern has been taken up efficiently by the propaganda machine of the Republican Party. A passage from the inaugural address of President Bush Senior in 1989 reveals how the blaming of the poor can be coated in a seemingly caring and compassionate language: "There are homeless, lost and roaming.... There are those who cannot free themselves of enslavement to whatever addiction—drugs, welfare, the demoralization that rules the slums. There is crime to be conquered, the rough crime of the streets".[15] Have you noticed that welfare is being depicted as an "addiction" and thereby directly associated with drugs, immorality, and *street crime*? We can see here how neoliberal ideologies penetrate and shape common sense images of poverty. In Newt Gingrich's Contract with America (1994) we read: "Government programs have bred illegitimacy, crime, ... and more poverty. Our Contract with America will change this destructive social behavior." We will eliminate the "culture of poverty" and replace it with a "culture of productivity."[16] Poverty, engendered on a mass scale by deregulation, deindustrialization, and race-to-the-bottom, has been transformed into a "behavior" to be cured by labor discipline.

It is one of the bitter experiences of liberals and progressives in the US that it was the Clinton administration that took the decisive step to implement this program. The Welfare Reform Bill of 1996 pushed the welfare recipients towards low paid jobs by curtailing their benefits. The Welfare to Work programs certainly caused a reduction of the number of the welfare recipients, but did not reduce poverty. Most of the workfare jobs were so poorly paid that they didn't help anyone climb out of misery. Even if the official poverty rates declined slightly in the late 1990s (due to the New Economy boom), extreme poverty (as measured by the "poverty gap" and rates of "poverty below half of the poverty line") has constantly deepened, as shown in Figure 6. Emergency food and shelter providers report a significant increase in the numbers of people they must help, most of them working poor: in New York City for example, most of those who depend on soup kitchens and food pantries are people with one or more jobs.

---

[15] Quoted after William DiFazio, *Ordinary Poverty. A Little Food and Cold Storage*, Philadelphia, 2006, p.2.

[16] ibid., 72.

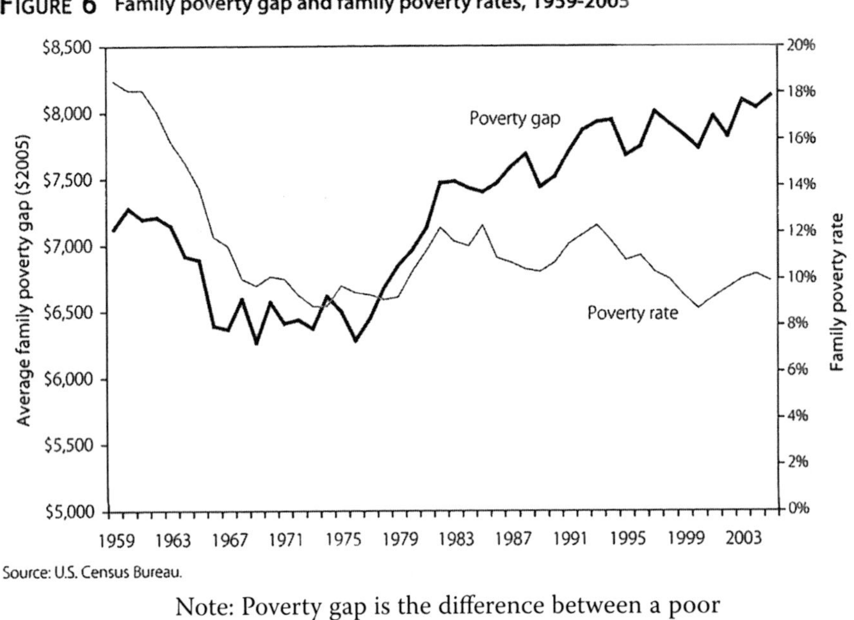

FIGURE 6 **Family poverty gap and family poverty rates, 1959-2005**

Source: U.S. Census Bureau.

Note: Poverty gap is the difference between a poor family's actual income and the poverty threshold.

No magical formula.

Are there any conclusions to be drawn in regards to our commitment to fight poverty? At first, my argument seems to complicate what we might have hoped was straightforward. If it is true that today's poverty cannot be separated from neoliberalism's philosophy and political economy, it cannot be overcome by charities and philanthropic initiatives that shy away from addressing this connection. If it is true that today's poverty is tied to the economic fabric of social inequality and injustice, election campaign promises to "end" it without questioning the underlying power relations are illusionary or misleading, at best. Without a broad social movement against poverty, led by the poor, not much will change. But as history shows, even the most vibrant movements are not protected against the danger of getting lost in the neoliberal maze of foundations and grant applications. The risk of being absorbed and losing stamina might be the greatest when they are successful.

No magical formula is at hand. What is needed, I think, is an organic combination of social movement(s) and a sustained critical analysis of the powers that be, on the economic, political, and ideological levels. This is not an academic critique as an end in itself. Rather this analysis focuses our attention on the mechanisms of systemic impoverishment and constructively works to transform people's common sense into an encompassing vision of social justice. This is where ethical discourses and "moral values" should focus, and social analysis can be a helpful intellectual tool in this task. We need to get engaged in the construction of a credible and appealing alternative to the still-prevailing market totalitarianism of neoliberalism—not by going back to an earlier Fordist stage of capitalism, but by creating new outlines and strategies suitable for today's high-tech economy.

Jan Rehman speaking at orientation
Union Theological Seminary
New York, NY
Photo: Paul Chapman

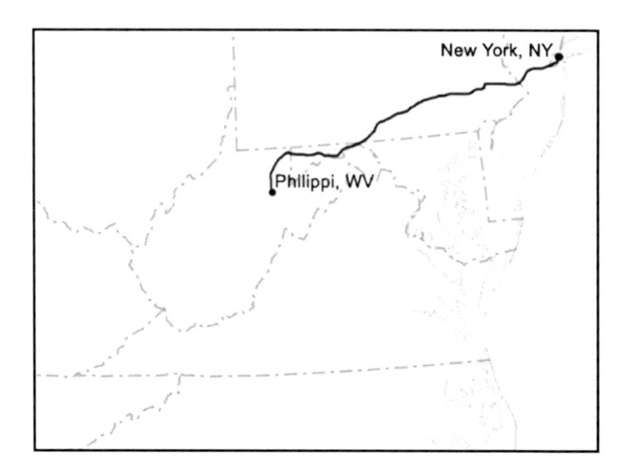

Sunday, January 7

Chapter 2

Itinerary:

Worship at the People's Chapel, located in Chestnut Ridge, Philippi, WV with Pastor Ruston Seaman

Lunch with World Vision-Appalachia and members of People's Chapel at the Chestnut Ridge Community Center, followed by conversations with area youth and community members.

Presentation by World Vision Staff on their mission and program

Dinner at the Philippi Baptist Church prepared by members of the group, led by Tallu Schuyler

Lecture by Appalachian Studies Professor Bill Klaus of Alderson-Broaddus College: "Explaining Appalachian Poverty: the history and politics of calling a place 'poor'"

Overnight at Alderson-Broaddus College

Tallu Schuyler (left) tells the group about the meal they are about to share as (left to right) Derrick McQueen, Paul Chapman and Liz Theoharis listen.
Philippi Baptist Church basement
Philippi, WV
Photo: Alix Webb

Professor Bill Klaus
Philippi Baptist Church
Photo: Jessica Chadwick

Interviews with youths at the Chestnut Ridge
Community Center
Philippi, WV
Photo: Colleen Wessel-McCoy

Immersion participants Lovelle Clark (top right), Eva Gordon (top middle), and Judith Scott (bottom left) with the youths they interviewed over lunch.
Chestnut Ridge Community Center
Philippi, WV
Photo: Alix Webb

Tallu Schuyler
Union Theological Seminary

Country Living

Jessica told us this morning that we would be going to a country church called People's Church here in Philippi, West Virginia. I couldn't wait for the wooden floors, the guitar music and the simplicity of the place. After arriving, I walked in to a newly renovated building to see lyrics of contemporary music projected onto a screen through Power Point. As the church band sang through the microphones, I noticed some of the walls were lined with Tyvek sheeting and many of the children wore T-shirts bearing the names of familiar television characters and state schools. This is a country church?

Country today is not what country was, but what ever was country anyway? What has been sold to me as perfectly country? I subscribe to a Condé Nast magazine called *Country Living.* The glossy publication offers me page after page of quaint interiors filled with antique fabrics and worn wooden furniture. It presents readers with photographs of empty, rolling land, lakes, rivers and running water that looks so easy to access. This is what I expect of country.

But having lived in rural East Tennessee, I know country is also crystal methamphetamine and Wal-Marts, poorly-funded public education and suburban sprawl, four-lane highways that lead to the mall, struggling farms and unemployment.

People with money have stolen the word "country," packaged it up and sold it to people like me, another person with money, who wants to look at pretty pictures. I want to believe that somewhere life still exists untouched by the damaging effects of globalization, capitalism, and environmental degradation. But on this second day of our trip, facing the realities of these mountains and talking with the people who live here, I realize the effects of such evils are impossible to escape.

Anyway, what is country living?

People's Chapel youths
Philippi, WV
Photo: Erica Almiron, Media Mobilizing Project

Several articles in *Appalachia: Listening With Our Hearts*, including Tallu Schuyler's "Country Living," were first published in the midst of our travel as online journal entries at http://povertyinitiativeappalachia.blogspot.com. We invited our churches, families and anyone on the world wide web to journey with us through these reflections. Suzie Francis discovered our blog and wrote the following response to "Country Living":

Hi Tallu,

I moved to rural WV when I was 8 yrs old and stayed until I was 30. I have visited often and was back there for a year recently (Sept 04-Oct 05). And you are so right—"country" is not what the rest of the world thinks it is. But, too, not all country churches are like the one you described. There are still churches where people still wear their "Sunday best" and sing from a hymnal with live piano or organ music, where they still use the King James' Version Bible and occasionally talk about Hell and Damnation.

As for your description of "country," and how it's being marketed, understand that there are people who have antiques, but they are usually antiques that are practical and still being used. We don't "collect" them for display; we use them. There are still people who cook from scratch—usually with ingredients straight out of their garden. They still bury their money in glass jars in the back yard. They are fiercely proud. They are old and tired and the younger generations are turning from the old ways.

Food stamps and Wal-Mart are easier than growing a garden and learning how to cook. We and our ways have been forgotten way too long. We have learned to live like the rest of the world--the easy way. And when that fails us, we don't know how to fend for ourselves anymore. And our pride comes from having a t-shirt with a popular character on it, not from knowing how to sew and make something ourselves. Pride comes from having the latest CD or DVD (even if it was bought from a vendor at a flea-market who taped it illegally) rather from having the ability to read, write, or make your own music. I don't know when this happened. Pride comes from having enough money to go to a fast-food restaurant for a sandwich with hard, white tomatoes and brown lettuce rather than from growing the biggest, reddest tomato in the county. But I feel partly responsible for not learning from my parents and grandparents and not carrying on the traditions.

I hope your team is visiting Appalachia to help them get that back and not to make them even more dependent on outsiders and their help.

Posted January 10, 2007 10:04 AM by "kuke"

Sara Suman and youth from People's Chapel play with a pup outside the Chestnut Ridge Community Center
Philippi, WV
Photo: Ellie Martin Cliffe

Youths from People's Chapel
Chestnut Ridge Community Center
Philippi, WV
Photo: Erica Almiron,
Media Mobilizing Project

Stefanie Schoen
Union Theological Seminary

Big Changes Will Come

Despite my expectation of the opposite, I really enjoyed the "charismatic" service we attended in the small country church on the hills. I liked the songs so much that I approached the singer after the service to ask for the lyrics. She introduced herself as Renata, and when she discovered I am German she asked, "I heard that my name is German, is it?" I replied, "Oh yes, it is common there, but it's actually Latin. It's such a beautiful name. Do you know what it means?" "What?" "It means 'reborn.'" She started to smile, her eyes filled with amazement, and said "Really? I felt this way since I was a child. I was the only one of eight brothers and sisters who knew the LORD. I used to play with him when I was a small child. And you know what? I know that big changes will take place here in this region. It will be such a big change that the world will learn to know about it. If we listen to what God wants us to do, we will know what our role will be."

Members of People's Church
Chestnut Ridge Community Center
Philippi, WV
Photo: Erica Almiron, Media Mobilizing Project

Liz Theoharis and youths from People's Chapel
Chestnut Ridge Community Center
Philippi, WV
Photo: Erica Almiron, Media Mobilizing Project

SELENE KAYE
Columbia University School of Social Work

A Warm Welcome

Yesterday we were welcomed by a community into their church to be with them as they worshipped. Members of the People's Chapel in Chestnut Ridge, WV made room in their small church for our group of 45 to join them and made time for each of us to introduce ourselves to them. I cannot imagine a greater gesture of warmth and hospitality than including us in such an intimate part of their lives and of their community. Especially because I didn't grow up going to church, it was amazing to me to be welcomed with such open arms into something so unfamiliar to me. People I'd never met treated me like a good friend, smiled and shook my hand with no trace of suspicion about who I am or why I was there. And although I do not believe the same things as they do, I found so much in the service to relate to: thinking about what our role in life is, taking responsibility for our own paths, dealing with anxiety, and focusing on the journey rather than on achieving success. I seek answers to these questions in different ways, but I felt a connection simply in the fact that we are all asking them. I felt admiration for the openness with which they seek answers.

We don't all agree on the answers, or the process by which they should be determined, and there is inevitably discomfort in being confronted by traditions and beliefs different from my own. I am feeling many things three days into our journey: excitement, curiosity, confusion, overwhelmed, connection, inspiration, exhaustion. But it is in the discomfort that I will be challenged to question my own beliefs and assumptions, and to grow and do the learning that I am here to do.

Two People's Chapel youths show Sarah Suman (center) the livestock
Philippi, WV
Photo: Erica Almiron, Media Mobilizing Project

Charon Hribar
Union Theological Seminary

Emmanuel—God Is With Us

The questions that I heard echoed several times today were—Where is God? And where do we look for God?

The "answer" that then followed on this Three Kings Sunday was—Emmanuel, God is with us. God is in our lives, in the midst of all that we are.

This was the spirit that I sensed emanating from the people whom I met today. From the sermons given by the pastors, to the friendly greetings of welcome we received from local parishioners, to the responses of Cody, a 10-year-old boy from Chestnut Ridge whom I interviewed at the World Vision Community Center, God's presence was real in the lives of the people.

But what does this mean for these people—what does it mean to say that God's presence is real? What responsibilities were made known in their understanding of God? In Cody's words, it's about making the world a better place.

Many of the people that we met in Barbour County today voiced the importance of community living. Pastor Ruston and others expressed the power of being in community and building genuine solidarity with one another in that community. He more specifically spoke to the need for people like us—social workers, ministers, and community leaders—remembering that the experience of living community should be much more a sharing relationship than a serving relationship. What was meant by this is that to work in community we must know that we are

Gayle Irvin with youth
Chestnut Ridge Community Center
Philippi, WV
Photo: Paul Chapman

not here just to help "others," but rather we must become a community and learn that we are helping one another. We must work to build relationships and recognize that we too are getting something back from these relationships. It is about humbling ourselves to move beyond the arrogance of charity and to embrace the possibility of sharing our lives with a community—and being changed ourselves.

My time in Barbour County left me with these questions: what would the world look like if we could learn to really be with one another? What does it mean to be truly in community with one another—to engage, listen, and share with one another? How do we move beyond our own assumptions, our own prejudice, our own fears, and our own self-preoccupation? It is in building community that I believe we will come to understand the spirit of the people whom we met today—to see the presence of God in our relationships, to see God where God is—in the midst of our daily lives, in all that we are.

Ben Cherland (left) and Dorothy Keith (right) engage with People's Church members after lunch
Chestnut Ridge Community Center
Philippi, WV
Photo: Colleen Wessel-McCoy

Immersion participants Stefanie Schoen (left) and Kumiko Kawasaki (right) talk with
two community members (center).
Chestnut Ridge Community Center
Philippi, WV
Photo: Colleen Wessel-McCoy

Chestnut Ridge Community Center
Philippi, WV
Photo: Erica Almiron, Media Mobilizing Project

Ellie Martin Cliffe
Union Theological Seminary

Complexity

Today's unseasonable West Virginia weather has paralleled my thoughts during these waking hours. My outlook was hopeful as I watched the sun rise over the hills, my first ever glimpse of the state of West Virginia in daylight. The rain started as the day drew on and we heard multitudes of stories about the joys and struggles of the people who live here. As the grass turned into fields of mud, my thoughts about our purpose for being here have changed and mixed with my reactions to what I've heard and seen in conversations with the people of Philippi. My preconceptions have all been proven wrong, and I'm thankful for that, but the complexity of all of this is much deeper than I could ever have expected.

Drew Paton (right) with youth from
People's Chapel
Chestnut Ridge Community Center
Philippi, WV
Photo: Selene Kaye

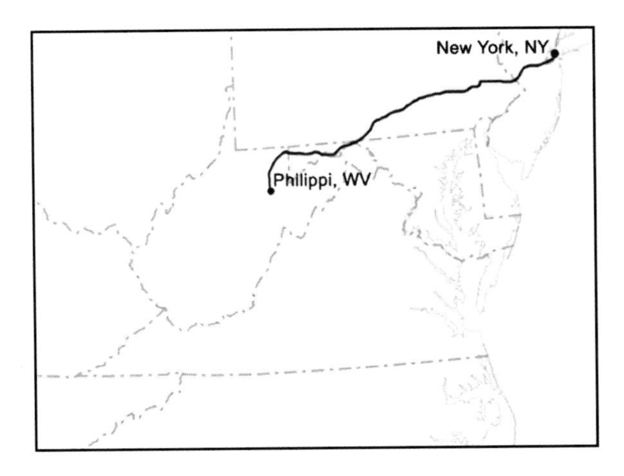

Monday, January 8

Chapter 3

Itinerary:

Biblical Reflection

Introduction to Head Start by the Media Mobilizing Project

Visits to area agencies:

West Virginia Department of Health and Human Services hosted by Beth Howard

Philippi Head Start hosted by Nancy Keller

Return to World Vision for lunch

Small group departs with World Vision staff to visit a youth center and help students with their homework at a middle school, rejoining the larger group for dinner back in Philippi

Presentation by World Vision staff Candy Adams and Chris Mullett on the Community Time Bank program

Divide into groups to volunteer with World Vision

- Work in the Warehouse
- Work in Chestnut Ridge Community Center basement
- Work in the Storehouse
- Help with Chestnut Ridge Kid Reach
- Conduct Time Banking Surveys

Dinner at Philippi Baptist Church

Art Reflection

Overnight at Alderson-Broaddus College

Immersion participants with Philippi Head Start host Nancy Keller
Philippi, WV
Photo: Sara Smith, Media Mobilizing Project

Head Start sign
Philippi, WV
Photo: Sara Smith, Media Mobilizing Project

Nancy Keller with Ben Sanders
Philippi Head Start
Philippi, WV
Photo: Sarah Smith, Media Mobilizing Project

Visiting one of the Philippi Head Start buildings
Philippi, WV
Photo: Alix Webb

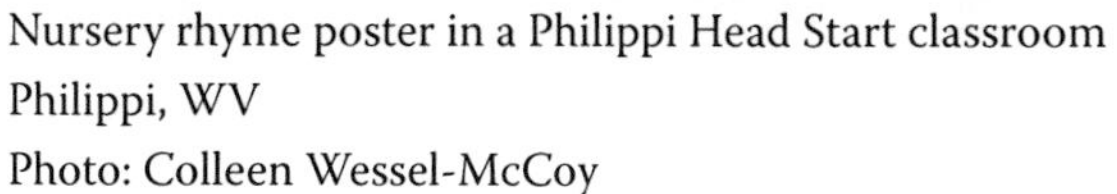

Nursery rhyme poster in a Philippi Head Start classroom
Philippi, WV
Photo: Colleen Wessel-McCoy

Ben Cherland (left) and Anne King (right) help prepare dinner in the Philippi Baptist Church kitchen
Philippi, WV
Photo: Ellie Martin Cliffe

Judith Scott
Union Theological Seminary

No Child Left Behind

> That the mountains may bring prosperity to the people,
> and the little hills bring righteousness.
> — Psalm 72

She was an active, enchanting little girl; nine years old—no—"I'll be ten next Monday"—with blond curly hair and the biggest blue eyes you could ever hope to see. Oh, she said, your hair's just like mine—and she grabbed my dreadlocks and squeezed them enthusiastically. Yes, it is, I said, and knew that we would be friends because curly-haired girls have to stick together.

I'd traveled along the Interstate, up the mountain, and over a river to get to her middle school with three other members of the Poverty Initiative.

Shaleen was working on a math worksheet.

Oh, yes. she said, I know this. The median, the mode and the range. See, first you put the numbers in order. Then you tick off the biggest number, then the smallest, then the next biggest like this.

Do you know what the median means?

Yes. You put them in order and then you.

OK. OK.

She went on with a completely mechanical set of operations, following the worksheet and getting the "right answers" as long as she did exactly what she was told in the order in which she was taught.

Where do you live—she asked me. New York City?

Those blue eyes widened, impossibly, and she said, Why???

Because that's where my parents are, I said.

Oh—she said. Did you come here to see me?

Yes. And other children here in West Virginia.

Maybe I'll go to West Virginia University. I want to be a vet. Because I love animals. And I hate to see them hurt.

Me, too. Do you have any animals now?

Well, we got some pigs. And I help take care of them. And I have a dog. I took care of her. When she was born she had a sack around her head. And she couldn't breathe. And we had to break the sac. But it wouldn't break when I pushed it with my fingers. So I had to use a pin. And then I had to rub her chest so she could breathe. And then we put her in a blanket and kept her warm and put—what do you call that needle?

An IV.

Yeah. And I watched that and took care of her for two days until she was strong enough.

I listened in amazement.

Our time is almost over, the supervisor said.

It was hard to say goodbye. For both of us.

Bye, Shaleen.

Bye. You write to me, she said.

Why had I gone to West Virginia? It was Epiphany; the time to remember to look for God in unlikely places. I certainly saw God's spirit shining through Shaleen.

I was glad that the after school supervisor, a local parent, was working for World Vision. She could make sure that someone saw beyond the worksheets and the drill. It's not just No Child Left Behind—but All God's Children—in the cities and in the mountains—living up to the full potential God has for them.

Stefanie Schoen helps a student with her homework at a middle school in West Virginia
Photo: Colleen Wessel-McCoy

Derrick McQueen (left), Drew Paton (right) and others volunteer in the World Vision warehouse.
Philippi, WV
Photo: Katy Moore

Paul Chapman
Poverty Initiative

Working Together to End Poverty

In the hills just south of Philippi, we took the winding road to Chestnut Ridge where we came to a cluster of buildings—offices, a community center, a warehouse and a chapel—headquarters of World Vision Appalachia, built to serve the surrounding area.

The services provided by World Vision are of significant value for many people who live very close to the edge of disaster. The Food Bank is most important. Much of the program is focused especially on children, and include after-school tutoring and mentoring. The children that we met appeared self-confident and hopeful about their future. For adults there is a warehouse selling low-cost building materials for home restoration, a time bank (you invest your time helping others and they receive proportional help in return) and a number of other services to improve the general welfare.

It is wonderful that the members of World Vision can live their faith by providing essential services to people of Appalachia. They seem to be people of deep faith, sustained by prayer and the promises of the Gospel. The language of faith is familiar to them. Surely the local people are inspired that World Vision staff and volunteers are able to express their Christian commitment in service to the world.

There is no question that World Vision is having a huge impact on the lives of the people in this area. The question is whether the indigenous cultural life of Chestnut Ridge and its surroundings

A member of the World Vision staff pointed out that our country equates your worth as a person with how much money you have and where you live. Poverty often brings on an overwhelming lack of self-worth and an immobilizing depression. He said that at World Vision Appalachia they frequently ask themselves, "What did the service I just provided do for the person's dignity and sense of purpose?"

Submitted by Colleen Wessel-McCoy

will be overwhelmed by World Vision with its staff of twenty and its $2,000,000 annual budget, a quarter of which comes from public funds through the government's faith-based "charitable choice" program.

During our travels I have learned a lot about the fierce loyalty of local people to their land, their traditions and their people. This cultural fiber has enabled the highlanders to push back against the values that threaten their land and their way of life. Economically, West Virginia is an occupied land—the economy controlled by outsiders; it is against these forces that the local culture represents a unique form of resistance. The "locals" of Chestnut Ridge embody a strong cultural and faith heritage that has sustained them for generations.

The staff of World Vision, most of whom are from outside the region, are very determined people, dedicated to raising the standards of living of the local people, while at the same time implanting a specific Christian message. The question that plagues me is whether World Vision, or any of us from "outside," will help local people release the immense power they have to confront the "colonial" structures that exploit them, or will we unwittingly impose a quality of life that pacifies and undermines the strength that we are witnessing in the local people?

In the terms of the Poverty Initiative, are we here witnessing the beginnings of a movement to end poverty, led by poor people whom we believe have the strength and the wisdom to move America out of its present injustice, if that strength can find release from the fetters which now bind it?

This question is especially hard since I, too, am an outsider, and I benefit from an economy that favors a few at the expense of the many. My comfortable life style is enabled by cheap West Virginia coal. Am I really willing to challenge the present economic arrangement? Are you?

So here's our challenge. How do we partner with Appalachians who understand the inherent injustice that plagues God's creation? They have experienced this injustice all their lives. What is our proper role, working with Appalachians for a world in which its resources are shared equitably by all—a land in which justice rolls down like waters and righteousness like an ever-flowing stream?

Immersion participants enjoy dinner prepared by a team of volunteers from within the group
Philippi Baptist Church
Philippi, WV
Photo: Gayle Irvin

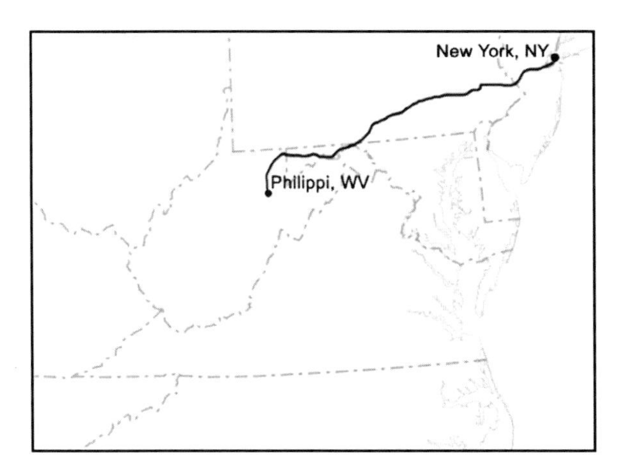

Tuesday, January 9

Chapter 4

Itinerary:

Textual Reflection

Walking tour of downtown Philippi with Dr. Danny Franke, Professor of Christian Studies at Alderson-Broaddus College.

Small group travels to Buckhannon, WV to spend the day at Upshur Cooperative Parish ("Parish House") hosted by Carol Duffield

Lunch and introduction to Parish House

Volunteer work

Conversation with Parish House staff and volunteers, including Union alumnus Marvin Carr, professor at West Virginia Wesleyan

Rejoin the group for dinner

Visit to Philippi Head Start for those who didn't visit on Monday

Charon Hribar (left), Paul Thorson (center) and Drew Paton (right) volunteer at Parish House Buckhannon, WV
Photo: Colleen Wessel-McCoy

Some return to World Vision for a driving tour of Chestnut Ridge with Candy Adams and Chris Mullett

Others attend lecture on the incarceration of poor women by Dr. Tom Horacek, psychologist at the Pruntytown Correctional Facility, professor of psychology, and former mayor of Grafton, WV

Dinner at the Philippi Baptist Church

Art Reflection

Prof. Danny Franke (right of center) shares Philippi's history with immersion participants gathered in front of the Philippi Covered Bridge during a walking tour of downtown Philippi
Philippi, WV
Photo: Colleen Wessel-McCoy

(front—right to left) Doug Duffield, Rev. Carol Duffield, Sarah Carr, Union alumnus Rev. Marvin Carr (back—left to right) Charon Hribar, Colleen Wessel-McCoy, Adam Barnes, a Parish House staff member, Jan Rehmann, two Parish House volunteers, Ellie Cliffe, and Drew Paton
Parish House, Buckhannon, WV
Photo: unknown

Doug Duffield moving gravel
Buckhannon, WV
Photo: Adam Barnes

Immersion participants Charon Hribar, Drew Paton, Adam Barnes and Ellie Martin Cliffe outside of Parish House.
Buckhannon, WV
Photo: Colleen Wessel-McCoy

(left to right) Jan Rehmann, Paul Thorson and Drew Paton
Parish House
Buckhannon, WV
Photo: Adam Barnes

Chestnut Ridge
Philippi, WV
Photo: Alix Webb

Eva Gordon
Columbia University School of Social Work

The Community Mainstay

For many years, if not centuries, the Church has been and still is one of the stable support systems that rural urban communities have depended on to fulfill their basic needs. Food pantries, child care, education and political leadership are just some of the basic services the Church provides in lieu of a caring government or society. World Vision Appalachia offers these services and others to the community of Philippi in West Virginia.

World Vision in Philippi has built a community center in the middle of Chestnut Ridge, a low income community nestled in the wooded hills outside of Philippi. At this center World Vision provides after-school tutoring and vocational training for young adults. They also have built a warehouse and stocked it full of donated building materials which can be purchased at minimal cost by the community. Rev. Ruston Seaman is pastor of the local church, People's Chapel, and has been largely responsible for integrating World Vision into Chestnut Ridge and the surrounding communities.

From my observation, Rev. Seaman has a vision for the people of Chestnut Ridge: to release the captives, free the oppressed and bring sight to the blind. The important question I had is; how does Rev. Seaman include the community of Chestnut Ridge in forming his vision of their community? One solution I saw is to hire people from the community.

Candy Adams is one such person. Candy is a native of Chestnut Ridge; she has been volunteering at World Vision and will begin full-time work

Tommy Goode from World Vision said churches populate communities, but rarely participate in community building. He envisioned churches measuring themselves on the basis of how well the community is doing, rather than how well the church is doing. Instead of operating budget or building size, benchmarks of success would be good schools for every child and access to health care for every resident, whether they are a member of the church or not.

Submitted by Colleen Wessel-McCoy

on one of its newest projects, a Time Bank, on January 15. Time Banking is a system of bartering whereby folks are able to offer their skills in exchange for credit or, "time dollars" which they can in turn use to purchase the skills of other community members. For example; one can give free piano lessons, earn several "time dollars," and then turn around and use them to buy gardening work from someone in the community who is offering that service. Candy will partner with World Vision's Chris Mullet on the Time Bank project. Chris is a native West Virginian, but comes from an upper middle class community forty miles from Chestnut Ridge. Although Chris admits he is an outsider in Chestnut Ridge, he has always envisioned himself working in Appalachia. One of the first things he told his wife when they got married was not to be surprised if he does ministry work in Appalachia. After eighteen years as a Baptist pastor he finally made his way to Philippi and World Vision about two months ago. Chris's goal is to eventually have Candy coordinate the Time Bank for all of Barbour County, which includes Chestnut Ridge, by herself. He would then start an additional Time Bank for Braxton County (a neighboring county of Barbour).

As part of the Time Bank project, Chris and Candy will have to interview people in the community and see what gifts they can contribute to the "social capital bank." Chris has made contact with very few people from Chestnut Ridge which is one of the reasons he is enlisting Candy's help. Candy is able to effectively communicate with both the folks of World Vision and the people of Chestnut Ridge. She is able to speak with them because she lives among them, these are her people and these are the people who World Vision intends to help. Who are Candy's people? They are natives of the Appalachian Mountain region, a poor, depressed area that many outsiders have mercilessly stripped of its natural resources. Candy and her people are of mixed heritage: European, African-American and Native American. So, not only do they struggle with life in a poor area, they also face the added challenge of being discriminated against for their mixed heritage.

Candy's goal in collaborating with Chris and World Vision is to get more of her people working as employees of World Vision. She hopes that not only will they work as kitchen help or janitors, but will also become coordinators and assume other significant roles at World Vision. Candy has said that in order to better understand how World Vision operates she put her skepticism to the test and volunteered with them. Now, as a full-time employee, she hopes to see if World Vision can fulfill its mission to help her community and her people.

There are many religious organizations and individuals who use the name of Jesus to abuse and take advantage of the poor. World Vision is not one of these. By working with Candy and in offering projects like the Time Bank, World Vision demonstrates that they are committed to building a strong, healthy, permanent community in Chestnut Ridge and Philippi.

World Vision staff Chris Mullett (left) and Candy Adams (right)
Philippi, WV
Photo: Alix Webb

WEDNESDAY, JANUARY 10

Chapter 5

ITINERARY:

Small group departs early to spend a day in Logan, Ohio:

Tri-county Community Action's Southeastern Ohio Regional Food Center (Second Harvest Foodbank and Meals-on-Wheels) and Head Start hosted by Dick Stevens and staff

Driving tour of Haydenville

Divide into two groups:

- Visit to Appalachian People's Action Coalition, hosted by Jerry Hartley
- Visit to Good Works, Inc. Hannah House, hosted by Keith Wasserman

Regroup to visit Athens County Jobs and Family Services in Chauncey, hosted by Jack Frech

Rejoin larger group in Athens for dinner

Lois Whealey, who arranged our day in Appalachian Ohio, shares lunch with us in the basement of the United Campus Ministries Center for Spiritual Growth and Social Justice
Athens, OH
Photo: Colleen Wessel-McCoy

John Winnenberg (left) shows Liz Theoharis a historic opera house origionally called The Red Men's Hall and now known as Tecumseh Theater, which Winnenberg and other community members plan to renovate.
Shawnee, OH
Photo and caption: Colleen Wessel-McCoy

Remaining group departs Philippi, WV and travels to Athens, OH

Small group has lunch at Episcopal Church of the Good Shepherd Free Lunch Program

Lunch at United Campus Ministries Center for Spiritual Growth and Social Justice

Lecture by Professor Bruce Kuhre, Ohio University

Travel to Trimble, OH

Introduction to Rural Action, hosted by Mary Steinmaus

Divide into small groups to visit organizations and projects that are part of the Rural Action network

Group 1: Chesterhill, OH

Hosted by Ada Woodson Adams, Bob Daugherty and Mildred T. Vore

- Henman Cave
- Opera House
- Library
- Quaker Meeting house and Cemetery
- Multicultural Genealogical Center

Group 2: Little Cities of Black Diamond

Hosted by John Winnenberg

- Rendville Art Center
- Shawnee theater
- SPiCYAM youth art center

Group 3: Essex Doser, Jobs Doser and New Straitsville, OH

Hosted by Mike Steinmaus

Monday Creek Restoration Project

Robinson's Cave

Community Revitalization and Park

Payne's Crossing

Regather for dinner at First Presbyterian Church of Athens provided by the church's Presbyterian Women's Group

Lecture by Professor Richard Greenlee, School of Social Work, Ohio University

Return to Parkersburg, WV to stay overnight at South Parkersburg Baptist Church

Mary Steinmaus (center) tells the group about Rural Action
Trimble, OH
Photo: Colleen Wessel-McCoy

At the Essex Mine discharge site whitish water pours off the hillside after picking up high concentrations of aluminum from passing through the old underground Essex Mine. The Essex Doser Project, part of the Monday Creek Restoration Project, treats the contaminated water.
St. Rt. 216 outside of New Straitsville, OH
Photo: Ellie Martin Cliffe
Caption: Colleen Wessel-McCoy, using "Little Cities of Black Diamonds microregion map, driving tour and directory."

Jan Rehmann
Union Theological Seminary

Interests Outside the Region

Central Appalachia was not "left behind" by the Industrial Revolution, explained Bruce Kuhre, sociology professor at the University of Ohio, Athens. Appalachia, he said, made the Industrial Revolution possible. It was an "internal colony," providing the rest of the nation with the raw materials it needed. At the heels of the lumber barons came the mineral hunters mapping out the sites for mining coal, oil and gas. A colonial economy, characterized by absentee ownership, 80% of the land and the minerals beneath it belong to "interests outside the region." The hills are gutted out. Families live in trailers. The abandoned mines spill their poisonous acids into creeks, streams, and rivers. I saw and smelled the foamy liquid exiting a mine cave, covering the stones with a white so shiny and artificial it reminded me of tooth paste ads. In nearby towns, the people sometimes turn on their faucets and find that their drinking water has turned rusty or black. In Appalachia I witnessed the devastation of people and nature alike.

Mike Steinmaus from the Monday Creek Restoration Project explains the water treatment process at the Essex Dosser
Photo: Peter Cava

Colleen Wessel-McCoy
Union Theological Seminary

"Relative" Poverty

The poverty that persists in developed nations is sometimes perceived as being less significant than poverty in developing nations—not just that poverty rates are lower (i.e. that there are fewer people who are poor) but that the poverty those poor people experience is less disconcerting. This is the implication behind comments such as, "in the US even poor people are over weight," "how can you be poor if you have a television set?" and "poverty in Africa is not having water; poverty in the US is not having designer sneakers."

Even some of the most well-known proposals for addressing global poverty ignore poverty in places like the US, calling it "relative" poverty in a "rich nation" and focus on "extreme" poverty in "poor nations." They argue that however little money you have in the US, you still have access to sanitary water, food, and basic medical services: Your tap water may not taste as good as filtered water, but it's always available and you can drink it without getting an infectious disease. You may get tired of PB&J or have to settle for whatever they're handing out at the food pantry, but you won't go hungry. You may have inferior health care, have to wait in long lines to receive it or be driven into bankruptcy trying to pay for it, but you won't die of a curable disease. You may have to share one room of a homeless shelter with 300 strangers, but you won't freeze to death. And in all of these cases, if you try hard enough, you won't have to make do with less for long.

Bruce Kuhre speaks at United Campus Ministries Center for Spiritual Growth and Social Justice as Peter Cava (left) listens. Athens, OH
Photo: Colleen Wessel-McCoy

Antrim Caskey took this photo of Kenneth Stroud at his home in Rawl, WV, saying "water from every tap in Kenneth Stroud's home in Mingo County came out rust colored, edged with a gritty oily substance some alleged to be diesel fuel" and that "Stroud has become seriously ill since he moved to Rawl."
Photo and quote:
www.clipfile.org/antrim

I've heard from people from all over the US whose experiences belie these myths, and Appalachia is no exception. When we arrived in Athens, Bruce Kuhre disabused us of one of the most basic assumptions: poverty in the US doesn't mean worrying about water. He showed us video clips of families whose faucets run with opaque dirty water. Women in the video spoke embarrassedly about getting unusual vaginal infections.

As a kid at camp in the mountains of North Georgia, I would fill my water bottle with untreated mountain spring water, so as I grew up mountains and clean water were synonymous in my mind. But mechanized coal mining produces tremendous amounts of liquid and solid waste, which is pumped back into the mountains. It is common for coal companies to pour it into the miles of old coal mines and then seal off the entrance. Communities that live in the valleys below these mountains find those chemicals in their drinking, cooking and bathing water.

Antrim Caskey describes the situation he found in Mingo County, WV:

> "The human costs of coal production are profound. The waste from coal mining and processing has poisoned the air and the ground water. I saw many people who had sores on their body from bathing in the poisoned water; anyone who can afford to buys all their drinking and cooking water, but most cannot. I felt like I was in a developing country brushing my teeth with bottled water."[1]

But Caskey also found that the citizens from Boone, Raleigh and Mingo Counties are fighting back. They turn out for public hearings on mining permits, telling state officials that "the air they breathe, the water they drink and the land they live on is making them sick and killing many," but they find a common refrain: "Thank you very much, we'll take your words [of protest] back with us." Instead of representing the interests of

[1] Antrim Caskey, "February 06, 2006: West Virginia Sacrificed for Our Thirst for Energy" www.clipfile.org/antrim. Accessed March 1, 2007

the residents, government officials settle permits in closed negotiations with coal companies. State resources are put towards reining in opposition to this corporate-state collusion: "State police are often present at the more controversial hearings, like those for expansion of the mine behind Marsh Fork Elementary in Sundial, Raleigh County."[2]

How we define poverty impacts the strategies we choose to pursue in ending poverty. Calling our attention to poverty in the United States is not an attempt to shift our attention away from the dire conditions globally, but to say that turning undeveloped nations into developed nations doesn't end poverty. Any analysis that fails to see the crushing reality of "relative" poverty is doomed to replicate it. Instead of artificial benchmarks that put poor people in competition with each other for being the most poor, the solutions to poverty lie in poor people themselves realizing how much they have in common across the borders of "rich" and "poor" nations.

[2] Ibid.

Antrim Caskey took this photo of Donnetta Blankenship who told him that she and her family "have been plagued with illness, poisoned by their contaminated water," yet the hollow in which she lives sits "between two multi-million dollar water projects and a golf course."
Photo and quote:
www.clipfile.org/antrim

Douglas Moore, Head Chef of the Food Bank's formidable kitchen gives us the tour of this immaculate facility. All of the staff we met at the Food Center impressed me with both their drive to feed their community as well as possible with whatever creative means they could and their deep connection to and compassion for the plight and fight of community members.
Logan, OH
Photo and caption: Alix Webb

Derrick McQueen
Union Theological Seminary

Hope

The night before, we had used all but the heelpiece of bread to stretch dinner for my Mom, my brother and me. Now we had officially run out of food and had nothing to eat. My mom had a great job at AT&T but as a single mother was left with all the debts, the car breaking down right before the rent was due and two boys she wanted to protect from it all. It was one of the first times I remember my mom really crying and not being able to stop. When I asked her what was wrong she told me that my little brother had just eaten the last bit of bread in the house. Even though we had lots of family in town, Mom was so sick and tired of borrowing a dollar here, some bread or milk there. Three to five dollars would have gotten us through the next couple of days but my mom was just beaten.

At the time I was thirteen, and I remember feeling so helpless. All I knew was that I didn't want my seven-year-old brother to see us like this. Mom agreed and apologized that I had to be a party to this. I told her it was okay. She showed me what she was holding in her hand. It wasn't just the bread that was gone; she was holding a gnarled and twisted tube of toothpaste that had been slit open from the bottom. There was not one bit of toothpaste left in the tube. Mom had put it on my brother's toothbrush so that he could brush his teeth. For her that was just the last straw. I started praying for our little family, Mom joined in and when we finished we both felt much better.

Food box
Tri-County Community Action Food Bank
Logan, OH
Photo: Alix Webb

I will be a forty-two-year old man in less than week. As I am writing this, tears are streaming down my face. You see, today I visited the Tri-County Community Action in Logan, Ohio that houses a Food Bank, Meals On Wheels and a Head Start program. As we toured the Food Bank they told us it had a full kitchen and a process to feed thousands. On distribution days people start lining up at 4 am to get their box of food, even though the facility doesn't open until 8 am. The line of cars stretches down the half mile driveway and then continues for several miles down the road. But people get food and get fed. This is not a report about the facility, I just wanted you to know how incredibly powerful it is to know that people who need food get it. It's simple, I know, but it means so much.

Canned goods
Tri-County Community Action Food Bank
Logan, OH
Photo: Selene Kaye

Learning that people here have banded together to do their bit to end poverty by feeding the hungry hit me hard and I am profoundly grateful. Tonight in Logan, Ohio there is a thirteen-year-old somewhere that doesn't have to watch his mother cry over her inability to feed his little brother. He won't have to carry that painful memory for the rest of his life. To me, that is a miracle. By the way, in the mail that day after Mom and I prayed and cried, a tube of sample toothpaste, or what I like to call hope, arrived in the mail. And things just seemed to get a little better. Hope came in the mail.

Dick Stevens (left) greets immersion particpants (left to right) Jason Seymour, Kim Komaszewski, Kary Moore, Drew Paton, and Jessica Pullido.
Tri-County Community Food Bank
Logan, OH
Photo: Alix Webb

Making fun of Appalachia stereotypes as well as pointing out the need for resourcefulness, Dick Stevens, our gracious host at the Tri-County Community Action Regional Food Center, shows us his technology/ingenuity to get messages from the reception desk on the first floor to his office on the second floor (a fishing rod with clothespin contraption).
Logan, OH
Photo and caption: Alix Webb

Gayle Irvin

Chesterhill

The trip to Chesterhill included a visit to the basement of a house believed to have been a stop on the trail of the Underground Railroad. We then drove deep into the woods to see caves that hid slaves until they could be ferried to safe places. It was a moving experience. I could sense the spirits of the people who came before and the horrific danger of their situation.

Multicultural Geneaological Center, the basement of which had been used to hide slaves on the Underground Railroad.
Chesterhill, OH
Photo: Sara Smith, Media Mobilizing Project

Risking the lives of themselves and their families, the Quakers of Chesterhill had hidden and ferried slaves. Their motivation was born out of their beliefs in social justice and equality. Though our visit to the basement and caves was a mere footnote in this long immersion week in Appalachia, for me the Quakers of Chesterhill serve as a model of a people whose actions were born out of their religious beliefs. They sought to simplify their lives to be free to serve others. They had a singular purpose in service—not to convert, but to do justice.

Immersion participants visit the Henman Cave
Chesterhill, OH
Photo: Sarah Smith, Media Mobilizing Project

Judith Scott
Union Theological Seminary

I come to you for shelter. *Protect me, keep me safe, and don't disappoint me. —Psalm 25:20*

A Psalm of David, when he had fled from Saul into the cave:

> *Have mercy on me, O God, have mercy on me,*
> *for in you my soul takes refuge.*
> *I will take refuge in the shadow of your wings*
> *until the disaster has passed.*
> —Psalm 57

We were driving through miles of countryside. "There were no roads here then. See—it's quite a way from the town." Our navigator and tour guide is Ada Woodson Adams, president of the Multicultural Genealogical Center in Chesterhill, Ohio, whose group is uncovering, publishing and celebrating the lives and stories of the people who lived and came through this part of the country in the early 19th century. The town, founded by Quakers, was a station on the Underground Railroad for runaway slaves, fugitives from their owners and from federal laws that considered them "stolen property." They had been sheltered and cared for on their journey North, from slavery to freedom. We were on our way to Henman Cave where runaways hid for days and nights, gathering strength and collecting provisions for the dangerous trip North. Today's townspeople had heard the stories about the cave and the people who stayed there. The stories were part of an oral tradition that seems as quaint and far away as the stories of the town founders. What was left was this cave and the Quaker Meeting House where decisions were made, plans were hatched, people prayed and discerned God's will.

"There are Amish farms around here now," our guide said. "But you won't see them. They're far from the road and they have their own schools. Sometimes you'll see the Amish families in buggies as they come into town or travel around the county." The countryside was beautiful. The road took us around curves that cut through the hills, bringing green fields into view, pastures and cultivated acres. From time to time isolated patches of trees appeared, leafless, shut down for winter—appropriate for this January day but incongruous given the green landscape of this impossibly warm 21st Century winter. We'd made friends with the hills on this trip; close enough to notice the differences between the sharp mountain clusters of West Virginia and these older, softer hills of Ohio that seemed to flow gently across the earth.

The cave itself was a stark gash in the mountain. It opened up high at the entrance and the ceiling lowered as you went further into its dark recesses. Looking out from the dark you could see the mountain in front and the sky above. The light and warmth of the sun did not reach inside. I was aware of two worlds at once—a warm bright outside full of promise and a cold, chilly inside where fugitives waited for Friends to bring them to freedom.

It wasn't until our return to New York City that I remembered a car ride to another shelter. Before we left for Appalachia we were driving from Manhattan, across the Triborough Bridge to Ward's Island and the city shelter, run by the Volunteers of America, where some of New York's homeless men spend the night on their journey from the netherworld of our society's so-called safety-net for the poor to decent housing and self-sufficiency. The road on the island seemed endless. How could this be New York City? The land on this winter day was flat and empty. In spring and summer this is park land for picnics and parties and relaxation away from the city streets. At one end there is a sports complex for track meets and circus spectaculars; at the other end are open acres with abandoned buildings. On and on we drove. Over the years Ward's Island has been the site for everything unwanted in the city: hundreds of thousands of bodies were relocated from the Madison Square and Bryant Park graveyards in earlier waves of urban renewal; sick and destitute immigrants were sent to The State Emigrant Refuge, a hospital opened in 1847. The New York City Asylum for the Insane opened around 1863 and immigrants landed here from 1860 until 1892 when Ellis Island opened.

Today, far away from the park and the stadium, there is a large mental hospital and this shelter. Hundreds of men sleep here each night. They are sent out each morning and must return by 10 p.m. to claim their bed. The dorm rooms look like wards with cement walls and linoleum floors. Each bed has a locker next to it and is separated from the next bed by a waist-high concrete wall. The bathrooms are open-tiled spaces with shower stalls, toilets and urinals. TV sets high up on the corridor walls blare commercials and a TV sit-com, watched by residents who are too sick or too old or disabled to be outside during the day. Fluorescent lights cast a sickly pall on the whole place. It smells of sweat and disinfectant, musk and endless waiting. The social workers and housing counselors whom we talked with told us how they meet with each man and make referrals for drug and vocational counseling. They provide support for "independent" living in SROs and apartments within thirty days. The counselors were upbeat and committed to their work. They were all leaving for the day as we left at about 5 o'clock. The shelter police—young men and women, black and Hispanic, locked in this isolated place with the "clients" every night and afraid for their safety and what, but for the grace of God, could well be their own future—looked at us with suspicion and defensiveness. Current and former residents of the shelter, members of Picture the Homeless, had spoken to us earlier in the day. They told us of being beaten by the guards, attacked by other clients, ignored by counselors, denied services, humiliated and abused.

Shelter bed and locker.
The shelter staff and the leaders from Picture the Homeless who had been residents there painted very different pictures of the same building.
Ward's Island, New York City, NY
Photo: Erica Almiron, Media Mobilizing Project

Is Ward's Island Shelter our present Underground Railroad? Are we providing a safe space for the poor on their way to a free and decent life? Will we bring visitors here one hundred years from now and proudly attest to our Christian witness—that we saw the hungry and fed them; that we saw the homeless and housed them? That would be sad. Because conditions there are grim. We run no risk supporting and aiding the homeless today. We are not breaking the law when we support organizations that are working to bring services and dignity to those who fall on hard times.

It's 2007. We can talk about the shelter and let everyone know it is there. We can invite Picture the Homeless into our Christian meeting house and learn about the shelters, and the anonymous burials on Hart Island. We can help today's fugitives, those escaping the chains of poverty, unemployment and homelessness. I traveled miles to Appalachia and years back into history and found that my sense of security in modern society's concern for the poor still depends on the efforts of active, caring people working together to assure dignity and justice. I found concrete ways to express Christian ethics today in my own hometown. Now that you've heard this and seen it—you know, too.

Among those buried in Payne Cemetery are Civil War veterans of the U.S. Colored Troops. Paynes Crossing was a small community settled by free Blacks who moved to the Ohio Territory in the early 1800s from Virginia.
Nelsonville, OH
Photo: Sara Smith, Media Mobilizing Project
Caption: "Point of Interest—Payne Cemetary" information sheet produced by Wayne National Forest Athens Ranger District, March, 2001

Rendville, OH
Photo: Colleen Wessel-McCoy

Andrea Roske-Metcalfe
Union Theological Seminary

Go to Rendville. Meet with the people there.
A sermon on the Directions to Rendville

> DIRECTIONS TO RENDVILLE
>
> Take State Hwy 13 north to Corning. After the 4-way stop, continue north to Rendville (about ¾ mile). After visiting with people at Rendville, go back to the 4-way stop. Turn right onto Hwy 155. Continue on 155 to Shawnee. At 4-way stop turn right into Shawnee and go up the hill.

One evening, during the Poverty Initiative immersion trip to Appalachia, we were told that there were four options for the following day in Ohio. Jess Chadwick gave us descriptions for three of them. They all sounded amazing: caves from the Underground Railroad, the Monday Creek Restoration Project, visiting a community made entirely out of clay houses. The final option, we were told, was a trip to Rendville.

(Silence)

"What's in Rendville?" someone finally asked.

"Well...we don't really know," said Jess, who had organized the entire course. "They didn't give us a description."

(Silence)

"OK, folks," Alix finally said. "We have to send at least one vehicle to Rendville." We all knew this, but none of us was particularly quick to jump at the chance.

I was sitting next to Colleen Wessel-McCoy, and I leaned over and said, "You know that it'll end up being the coolest trip."

"Yeah," she replied, "the ones with no information always are."

"You want to go to Rendville?" I asked her.

"OK," she answered, "if you go to Rendville."

We turned out to be a motley crew of martyrs – Colleen, myself, Jess Chadwick, Liz Theoharis, and her partner, Chris Caruso. Every single one of us, except for Chris, is employed by the Poverty Initiative. We simply went to Rendville because no one else would.

A few minutes after we had left, it occurred to me to actually look at the directions we had been given by Rural Action, the non-profit that organized our trips that day. When I did, I realized that rather significant portions of the directions were missing. We go right from "continuing north to Rendville" to "after visiting with the people at Rendville..." There was absolutely no information on this piece of paper to give us any indication of where to go once we got to Rendville, or who it was we were supposed to meet with in the first place!

We spent the next ten minutes making fun of these directions, saying "Go to Rendville. Meet with the people there," in sarcastic, romantic voices, and thinking about where we might find these people in Rendville. (Should we go door-to-door? Should we go to the supermarket? What if no one in Rendville wanted to talk to us?) Colleen hoped aloud that there was a Dairy Queen in Rendville, so we could meet with the people *there*. After three-quarters of a mile, as the directions said, we found a frontage road, with a burned-out trailer and a few other buildings that had obviously collapsed years ago.

"You guys think this is it?" Chris asked.

"If it is, I don't think we'll find anyone to visit with," said Jess.

We drove for another thirty seconds and found a little gathering of about ten buildings, two of which were churches. We turned off the highway and drove down the road, and saw that one of the churches had been renovated into an art gallery, with brightly colored signs and stained-glass sculptures hanging in the windows. Everything else was either boarded up or a private home. If this wasn't where we were supposed to be, then it really wasn't our fault.

We didn't even make it to the door before a man in paint-spattered work clothes and a wide smile opened it, and said, "You're late! I've been waiting for you guys for an hour!"

Go to Rendville, indeed. This man's name was John Winnenberg. He had grown up in the next town over, was a local historian, and had founded an artists' collective for people with disabilities.

For the next few hours we sat, surrounded by paintings, sculptures, and stained glass, and learned all sorts of things that we never would've expected about this tiny little town called Rendville. This church-turned-art gallery was home to a religious revival in 1885, organized with the purpose of ridding the town of drunkenness and gambling. A man named Adam Clayton Powell, Sr. walked past that church during a revival. He thought it sounded interesting, and went inside. He found Jesus in that church, and went on to become the minister of the Abyssinian Baptist Church, just up the road from us in Harlem, the largest African-American congregation in the country.

(left to right) Andrea Roske-Metcalfe, Chris Caruso, John Winnenberg, and Liz Theoharis in front of the church where Adam Clayton Powell, Sr. found Jesus. Rendville, OH
Photo: Colleen Wessel-McCoy

Rendville was the first town in Ohio to elect a black mayor. Black leaders in Rendville organized in the 1880s to form the Afro-American League. By 1887 they had struck down laws that separated black and white children in schools and that prohibited interracial marriage. Blacks and whites co-existed in Rendville long before they did in almost every other place in the US

The Knights of Labor was the very first labor union formed by miners, and it was organized by the miners in Rendville, along with others in nearby towns. They built an opera house for their meetings. John took us there. It looks like the underwater photos of the Titanic – you can imagine the operas and what the people in the audience must have been wearing, you can feel the energy of those early union meetings, even while you have to be careful not to step through the floorboards.

Go to Rendville. Meet with the people there.

We like directions, in our culture. We like detailed maps, address numbers, and hopstop.com. We like specifics. We don't like to be lost. We're uncomfortable with ambiguity, especially in directions. After all, we go to specific places in order to do specific things, and to meet with specific people. We like reason and logic.

Rendville Art Works, a folk art gallery and studio for local artists.
Rendville, OH
Photo: Colleen Wessel-McCoy

Go to Rendville. Meet with the people there. It sounds…presumptuous, doesn't it? Can you imagine these cryptic directions anywhere else? Go to the Bronx. Meet with the people there. Go to Seattle. Meet with the people there. Go to Darfur. Meet with the people there. It's so big. It's so wide open. We could meet anyone. Does it even matter who we meet? Does it matter where we go? Does it matter…if we go…at all?

Go to Picture the Homeless. Meet with the people there. Go to the spa on Madison Avenue. Meet with the people there. Go to the laundry room. Meet with the people there.

We like directions in our culture, but we also like safety. We like to know what we're getting ourselves into, and we tend to avoid situations where we're not exactly sure how things might go. So we don't cross a lot of boundaries. We don't seek people out if we don't know who they are. We'd really rather talk *about* them, than talk *with* them.

Rendville Art Works
Rendville, OH
Photo: Colleen Wessel-McCoy

Go to Rendville. Meet with the people there.

It's a big, wide-open invitation. We have a tendency to talk about important issues in big, wide-open terms, too, but they tend to have the opposite effect. We use big words—words like "wealth," and "poverty." It's easier this way, you see; we feel like we have the whole picture, and we can look for big, far-reaching solutions. We like solutions, in our culture. We like to tie up loose ends.

But these big words skip over a lot of important things. They skip over Rendville. They miss the innovative ways that the people in a tiny little town in Ohio banded together to demand higher pay for dangerous work. They miss the fact that the Civil War *did* mean something in some places, and that the things Martin Luther King, Jr. dreamed about where already a reality, in some places. Rendville is basically a ghost town now. These big words of ours miss the fact that this town's amazing history of seeking justice for its people is about to be lost, because there isn't any money, in this shell of an old mining town, to preserve it.

The big picture, with its far-reaching solutions, skips over Rendville, and the things we'll learn about the people there, and about ourselves in the process. If all this history, if all these lessons can come from ten little buildings, then how much more must we be missing when we use big words to describe the people in the Bronx? How much must we be missing when we describe the people just about *anywhere*?

Go to Rendville. Meet with the people there. We did. We didn't do it because we're such wonderful people. We did it because someone had to, and no one else would go. I had a bad attitude; I'll admit it. I half-hoped that we *could* just go to the Dairy Queen, and meet with *one another* there! I doubted that Rendville had much to teach me that I didn't already know.

I didn't choose to go to Rendville. If I had had a choice, I would've gone to see the clay houses! I went to Rendville because I had to. And I'll try to remember that, the next time someone asks me to go somewhere that doesn't sound very interesting; somewhere where I think I already know everything that the people there could possibly have to teach me. I'll try to remember that the big picture doesn't help much unless we know the stories...unless we know the people.

Go to Rendville. Meet with the people there.

Andrea Roske-Metcalfe (left) listens as John Winnenberg (right) shares some of Rendville's African-American history. Residents included Rev. Adam Clayton Powell, Sr.; Black labor organizer Richard L. Davis; the first Black mayor in the North, Dr. Issaiah Tuppins, who was also the first Black man to earn a medical degree in Ohio; Sophia Mitchell, Ohio's first Black Woman mayor; and Roberta Preston, the first Black Woman Postmaster of the US Postal Service.

Rendville Art Works

Rendville, OH

Photo: Colleen Wessel-McCoy

Caption: Colleen Wessel-McCoy, using "Little Cities of Black Diamonds microregion map, driving tour and directory"

John Winnenberg (center) tells (left to right) Liz Theoharis, Chris Caruso, Jessica Chadwick and Andrea Roske-Metcalfe about historic Shawnee, whose overhanging porches and unique architecture make it one of the best standing examples of a turn-of-the-century boom town in the eastern US.
Shawnee, OH
Photo and caption: Colleen Wessel-McCoy, using "Little Cities of Black Diamonds microregion map, driving tour and directory."

Ben Cherland
Union Theological Seminary

"You Can't Go Home Again" –Thomas Wolfe

Professor Rich Greenlee spoke to our group in the basement of First Presbyterian Church in Athens, Ohio, after a long day of travel and learning. He tells people his story, as he told us, in hopes of dispelling the stereotypes people hold of native Appalachians. This is his story, as I heard it, and my reflections on it.

Rich Greenlee was born in the hills of West Virginia to a poor family. He was one of six children. His father was a coal miner, and they struggled to get by. They collected welfare and eventually needed to use food stamps to feed everyone. At one point the whole family had to move into a barn on a friend's property. They didn't have running water or electricity. Rich lived in fear that his classmates at school would find out how he and his family lived.

To his own surprise, he graduated from high school, and shortly thereafter joined the military. He said, "It would be better than staying here." In the military he had a commanding officer who took an active interest in his well-being. This man got Rich started in college, refused to let him quit, and supported him through it all until Rich had the degree. Rich was the first person in his family to go to college. He might very well be the last.

My mother, Meredith, was born in Providence, Rhode Island to a working class family. Her father was just out of the service when she was born in 1947. My aunt Joyce was born four years later. While their mother had a high school diploma, Grampa had little more than a tenth grade edu-

cation and a record of service. Still, this family of four, with two parents working full-time, barely managed to get by.

When mom was eleven the whole family packed up and moved to Stratford, Connecticut. They lived on the end of Linton St., on the edge of a forest, with the Merritt Parkway going through their backyard.

My mother tells me that she grew up in a loving family that never had much, but enjoyed it when they did. When they had the money, Nanna would use her lunch break to shop for clothes for the girls or Grampa would take them all into the city for dinner and a show. But these opportunities were rare.

Because they chose to spend the little extra money they made rather than save it, things got tight at home when it came time for my mother to go to college. They never lived "paycheck to paycheck" but it was close. She went to the University of Connecticut in Storrs and was the first person in her family to go to college; her parents were very proud.

Rich Greenlee went on after college and the military to earn other degrees. He went to other schools, met new people and got married. His degrees and interests in social work eventually led him to Athens, Ohio where he now teaches in the Social Work department and holds the title of Associate Provost for Appalachian Access and Enrichment Programs.

After finishing college in Connecticut, my mother moved to Boston with some of her sorority sisters and taught in the Boston Public School system, later returning to school and earning a Masters degree from Boston College. She moved again, this time further away than ever before. Colorado needed teachers and she wanted to teach. This is where she met my father.

Part I

They left their land and their people...

My mother left because she felt like she no longer belonged. And she wanted to experience other parts of the country and the world that had been introduced to her in college and graduate school. Her education and her subsequent interests in feminism and social justice gently alienated her from her family and the socioeconomic class and culture of which her family was a part. She wanted to fight unfair systems and work for justice, and she felt as though she could only do so by leaving.

Rich left because he did not want to stay. He had experienced the reality of poverty with his family, its constant assault on their dignity, and he had had enough. He knew that if he stayed he would be doomed to a low paying, labor-intensive job and eventually marry someone and settle down just like his peers. As he saw it, the only option was leaving, and that worked out just fine. He figured he would eventually come back, but he knew he did not want to stay.

But they did not belong.

My mother cried as she and my father drove into Saskatchewan for the first time. My father, who had grown up there, was visiting for a job interview. Though it was April, there were no flowers, the trees still had no leaves, and the city seemed to be all grey and brown. It was the ugliest place my mother had ever seen.

Dad got the job, they settled in and Mom eventually came to see the beauty of this alien land. The people were kind and generous as well, but Mom knew she did not belong: She was different from everyone, as her east coast American accent was quick to tell.

Rich's accent gave him away as well. His peers in the military and in college would say, "You sound funny." He tried his best to cover up his West Virginia accent by masking it or by not speaking at all. He had few friends in those years and was generally treated as an outsider.

They found a world plagued by injustice...

In the military, Rich felt he had more in common with his African- and Latin- American peers than with middle class white men. In college too, he sensed deep injustices existing in society. He grew in this consciousness and was drawn to the field of Social Work. He earned a masters degree, then a doctorate, in an effort to learn about injustice and to help the afflicted.

College campuses were exciting places in the 1960s and my mother was in the thick of it. The Civil Rights Movement was underway and the women's movement was taking off with great speed. She grew in understanding and found that the world was a better place for some than it was for others. She wanted to work to change that.

And upon returning to their land and their people they found they no longer belonged.

Not long after Rich had left, his father died of Black Lung from his coal mining days. Rich often went home to visit his mother and his siblings, and when he did his family would say, "You sound funny." His vocabulary was different; he was sounding more and more like his peers in the military and in school. While his accent kept him on the social periphery at school and in the military, he found that it was now alienating him from his own family.

He also felt a sense of guilt. He was the only one of his brothers and sisters to leave the area. He was the only one to get an education. He was the only one who was no longer poor.

Mom would return home often as well, eventually with her new family in tow. I spent many Christmases in that house on Linton Street as a young boy. But she too felt like an outsider. She described first having this feeling in college: home for breaks she would find that she had less and less to talk to her family about. Once fully entrenched in a career, with another family in a different land and culture, she sensed they shared even less in common.

Part II

Though there are many parallels, the stories of Meredith and Rich are actually quite different, starting with the difference between growing up working class and growing up working poor. My mother's family always had enough to eat, electricity, water, a home, cars, etc. Rich's did not. Indeed, due to their lower socio-economic class, there were many ways in which Rich and his family suffered more than my mother's family did.

Another difference is that Rich was not a woman. My mother grew up and went to college in the 1950s and 60s. This was a time when women were just beginning to throw off the bonds of patriarchy and redefine themselves. The country was changing rapidly at that point but it was still a time of outright and overt sexism and discrimination based on gender. It was an exciting time to be a woman, but it was certainly not easy. My mother's gender put her at a greater disadvantage than Rich's gender did.

One final but important difference in their stories is geographical. My mother was from New England, a very privileged part of the country. This region has benefited from a historical and economic legacy that has kept it, to a certain degree, relatively unexploitable. Appalachia on the other hand has suffered from attacks on many fronts throughout its history: From the stereotypes of its people developed by the local color writers of the early 20th Century, to the ecological legacy of absentee land ownership, to the political and economic interests that have ravaged its land and its people. This is a region that has suffered immensely and a people who are marked by that suffering and stigmatized for it. Rich's origins put him at a greater disadvantage than my mother.

Despite all the differences, one thing remains binding: chance. It was only by chance that my mother's parents remained healthy and able to work, did not have massive hospital bills to pay, or fall into debt. Any one of these things might have put them over the edge into poverty. It was only by chance that Rich was physically healthy enough to join the military after high school; that he ended up under the command of that particular officer who helped him get that college degree.

Privilege is important to understand and to be aware of, particularly for the privileged themselves. Privilege and disadvantage played a significant role in the life of both Meredith and Rich. I believe that perhaps chance played a more central role. Though we must always remain aware of the realities of privilege and opportunity, we should not ignore chance. Concentrating only on privilege, I keep myself at a comfortable distance from the growing numbers of poor persons and families in this country, mistakenly believing that no matter how much I choose to care about the unprivileged, I never have to worry that I could be one of them, because I am privileged. The possibility that chance plays a more central role than privilege in deciding who gets by and who does not tears down a false divide that has been erected between the not-currently-poor and the poor, uniting both sides in our shared vulnerability. Just as the stereotypes we have of the poor whites of Appalachia that tell us their poverty is their own fault (due to laziness, stupidity, ignorance, etc.), our emphasis on privilege sets up walls between us that keep us from truly engaging in the responsibility we have for each other.

If chance is indeed a more significant factor than we usually give it credit for in deciding who succeeds and who slips into poverty, we have perhaps found an even deeper motivation for changing a system where people are denied the support they need to survive the challenges chance can bring: After all, *it could have been me and I could be next.*

Immersion participants hike up to Robinson Cave, a sandstone outcroping above downtown New Straitsville. Coal minners held secret meetings here, out of which they formed the United Mine Workers Union in 1890. Among them was Chris Evans, who became nationally known as a labor organizer. In 1884 miners met at the cave to plan the Great Hocking Valley Coal Strike, which included setting undergound mine fires that have not been fully extinguished even today.
New Straitsville, OH
Photo: Adam Barnes
Caption: Colleen Wessel-McCoy, using "Little Cities of Black Diamonds microregion map, driving tour and directory," produced by the Little Cities of Black Diamonds Council, Shawnee, Ohio. www.littlecitiesofblackdiamonds.org.

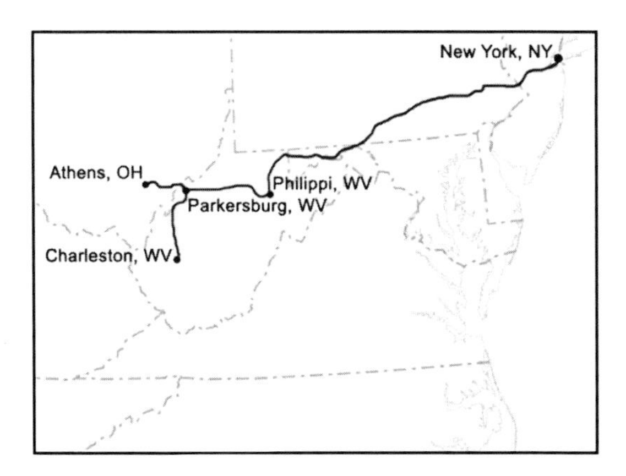

Thursday, January 11

Chapter 6

Itinerary:

Biblical Reflection

Travel to John XXIII Pastoral Center, Charleston, WV for a day hosted by Direct Action Welfare Group (DAWG) and West Virginia Council of Churches (WVCC), including presentations by:

Evelyn Dortch, DAWG

Rev. Matthew Watts, WV Workforce Investment Council

Samuel Hickman, National Association of Social Workers, WV

Rev. Dennis Sparks, WVCC

Bishop Bernard Schmitt, Wheeling-Charleston Diocese

Dinner at restaurant in Charleston, WV

Return to Parkersburg, WV to stay overnight at South Parkersburg Baptist Church

Rev. Matthew Watts told us poor Black people are "in the same boat with poor whites, poor white people just don't know it."
Charleston, WV
Photo: DAWG
Caption submitted by Colleen Wessel-McCoy

(left to right) Bob McConnell, Patricia Wray, Evelyn
Dortch and Sharron Witherspoon (front) of DAWG
Charleston, WV
Photo: Sarah Smith, Media Mobilizing Project

Chris Grove

Running with the Big DAWG

Seven poor West Virginians working hard to play by the rules of the game started the Direct Action Welfare Group (DAWG). In a game of incredibly unequal odds, whose leading players are seemingly more concerned with their own wealth and power than with the lives of other persons, the rules were again changing. In 2001, Evelyn Dortch and six fellow students were trying to complete a college degree in West Virginia, when deeper cuts to welfare—intended to deny access to any university student—were announced. Most of the original founders of DAWG were struggling to raise families in a housing project, where their children were automatically labeled as 'special needs,' securing more money for the public school without any additional assistance for their children. A college degree was meant to be the key step to a new, economically secure future, but pending welfare cuts would deny Evelyn and her friends the temporary support that had ensured basic necessities for them and their families. Declaring, "We are the current and former welfare recipients and people in poverty who struggle everyday to create change in our communities," DAWG successfully organized to ensure that West Virginia remained one of the few states to allow college education to count towards 'welfare-to-work' requirements.

Within the US, West Virginia has often been treated and described as an internal colony, its people impoverished despite grueling work in dangerous conditions while outside corporations profit from the exploitation of its natural resources in coal and timber. New mining technology and factory closings have led to unemployment rates of over fifty percent in some counties, making Wal-Mart the largest employer in the state. Under West Virginia's new motto 'Open for Business,' the Wal-Mart in the town of Nitro was given a fifty-year tax break; however, neither Wal-Mart's employees nor those displaced by Wal-Mart will be guaranteed a living wage, childcare, or health care. The exploitation of West Virginia has long been justified by the proliferation of degrading stereotypes about 'white trash' and 'hillbillies;' while throughout the US, the poor, often forced onto welfare by factory closings or wages inadequate to afford rent or health care, have been dehumanized, depicted in narrow racial terms, and labeled with pathologies. Yet Evelyn explained that the average welfare recipient in West Virginia is a 32-year-old, white woman with two children, who has been on welfare for two and a half years. Repeatedly we met hardworking, articulate persons, who cared for and supported one another based on connections of family, friendship and community. In meeting Evelyn and other members of DAWG, including Patricia Wray, Sharron Witherspoon and Bob McConnell, we had the privilege of learning from grassroots leaders who are committed to organizing to ensure the rights of people in their community and throughout West Virginia.

Evelyn Dortch of DAWG
Charleston, WV
Photo: Sara Smith, Media Mobilizing Project

As we continue to work together to build a movement to end poverty, DAWG offered several valuable lessons. The leaders of DAWG spoke with clarity, commitment, and legitimacy, as persons who had collectively questioned and challenged the injustices of poverty, unemployment, welfare cuts and housing policies. While the organization is primarily led by those directly affected by poverty, DAWG has welcomed the participation of all those committed to ending poverty and ensuring rights to education, health care and a reasonable standard of living. In particular, they have formed alliances with the National Association of Social Workers and with multiple churches, several of whom were invited by DAWG to meet with us. DAWG has worked strategically within their particular cultural and political context. With a population of only 52,000 in Charleston, politicians are accessible, and thoughtful discussion often leads to change. However, DAWG has realized the importance of being able to mobilize persons to undertake collective direct action, ensuring that their voices are heard. Their membership has been built by educating persons about their rights, supporting challenges to injustice in specific communities while connecting these to wider struggles to end poverty, and demonstrating the power of collective action.

DAWG recently celebrated the increase in the federal minimum wage, partly due to their advocacy with West Virginia's Congresspersons. However, the right to education is again being threatened. Under the new Budget Deficit Reduction Act, the federal government has announced that college education will no longer fulfill work requirements associated with welfare. DAWG members are mobilizing to demand that over 500 welfare mothers currently registered in West Virginia colleges, as well as future generations, will be able to exercise their right to education. DAWG is also eager to fight developments in a new West Virginia Medicaid law that will force recipients to sign and follow 'personal responsibility contracts' or face a reduction of health care benefits for themselves and their children. Ultimately, we need to build a nationwide movement to guarantee the economic human rights of all persons in every state, connecting our struggle with the poor worldwide who are impacted by similar economic policies and rules of the game. I am excited to be part of building this movement to end poverty with DAWG, grateful for their example and leadership.

Haydenville is known as one of southeastern Ohio's last company towns. Worker's houses were constructed using locally made brick. Different shaped houses denote different ethnic / racial backgrounds of occupants
Haydenville, OH
Photo and caption: Alix Webb

Kim Tomaszewski
Union Theological Seminary

What Will the Righteous Do?

Bishop Bernard Schmitt, one of several speakers we heard Thursday afternoon at the John XXIII Pastoral Center, focused his talk on Psalm 11:3: "If the foundations are crumbling what will the righteous do?" Before reading it he made a point of saying that he was using the New Revised Standard Version, the translation I normally use. Impacted by the passage, I went to underline it in the travel Bible I had with me—a New International Version—and discovered my translation read, "When the foundations are being destroyed, what can the righteous do?"

How does this small shift in language change what this verse says about responsibility? About the privilege of choice?

That morning in biblical reflection we had talked about themes in Ruth that paralleled the situation of coal miners here in Appalachia and poor people in general, specifically that being poor affects your having—or not having—choices. Ruth is dependent on Boaz for the survival of the next generation, for her well-being, and for her mother-in-law's well-being. People who work in the coal mines are thought of as expendable: dying early and cruelly, working in terrible conditions, being forced out of education into labor, and often having to bring their family into this line of work to face the same. But they must work in the coal mines in order to support their family—in order to survive. What is the difference in hearing "What *can* you do" versus "What *will* you do"?

This has been the crux of my experience with the Poverty Initiative: being presented with information, hearing people's testimonies, experiencing things with poor people, and then being asked, "Ok, now what will we do about these crumbling foundations?" We must understand our responsibility to one another and to ourselves as connected to one another, and we must do something about our crumbling foundations.

Rev. Matthew Watts told us that West Virginia has one of the lowest crime rates and one of the highest prison rates. He said this stems from the loss of jobs to the mechanization of coal mining: Prisons are the U.S. solution to poverty and excess labor.

Submitted by Colleen Wessel-McCoy

If I leave this trip with nothing else it will be the dichotomy of how immensely poor this region is but how hard people work. We have seen the working poor everywhere. It is exasperating to know that Wal-Mart is the largest employer in West Virginia. After driving out Mom and Pop stores they make the same people work in their stores for lower wages because there are no other options. People work with low or no benefits, awful pay, and long hours, and still, we stereotype them as being lazy. We place the blame of poverty on poor people themselves so we can live without guilt.

I went to college in central Pennsylvania. The relationship between my school and the community that surrounded it was not a positive one. We were middle to upper class white students who called the town "ours" for the four years we spent there, but did not appreciate the working poor that supported our late night Wal-Mart runs, deli stops and bar nights. Last night Prof. Greenlee said "It is great that you want to help and that you give cans of food, but if you really want to make a differ-

Bishop Schmidtt (standing center), Bishop Emeritus of Wheeling-Charleston, speaks to immersion participants at the John XXIII Pastoral Center
Charleston, WV
Photo: Colleen Wessel-McCoy

ence, say hello to the cashier." I keep coming back to this element of responsibility: understanding who is around us in our community (our state, our country, our world) and acknowledging our connectedness to them. What will we do as the foundations are crumbling?

A portion of a theatre movie projector in the old Opera House Chesterhill, WV
Photo: Sarah Smith, Media Mobilizing Project
Caption: Paul Chapman

Colleen Wessel-McCoy
Union Theological Seminary

"An Act of Man"

"The Buffalo Creek Flood,"[1]
(Written by Doug Yarrow and Ruth Yarrow, with music adapted from Woody Guthrie's "1913 Massacre")

In Logan County where coal is the King,
Where the people work hard for most everything,
On Buffalo Creek it was cloudy and gray,
And the people were rising to meet a new day.

The bacon was sizzling, the coffee was poured,
But the dam up the holler couldn't hold any more.
And the water raged down, smashed town after town.
Homes dashed to pieces and whole families drowned.

How could it happen? How could it be?
That dam it belonged to the coal company.
An "Act of God" the bosses did cry.
But God ain't that cruel, we can see through your lie.

Who ordered the dozer to build that dam?
And who's living high off the work of our hands?
Who takes out coal but don't share in the fear?
And who's greed for money has cost us so dear?

Yes, who's greed for money has cost us so dear?

Samuel Hickman from the National Association of Social Workers sang this song for us during our time together at the John XXIII Pastoral

[1] *Buffalo Creek Flood: An Act of Man.* Accessed February 2007 at www.appalshop.org/buffalo/media/BCF-transcript.pdf .

Center. He told us it was based on a true story, the details of which I learned from a transcript of the documentary, *The Buffalo Creek Flood: An Act of Man.*

On February 26, 1972 in Logan County, West Virginia a coal-waste dam collapsed, dumping over 132 million gallons of water and one million tons of sludge into sixteen communities along Buffalo Creek, killing 125 people and leaving 4,000 homeless.

Shirley Marcum, whose house was riped off its foundation and floated into a neighbor's house recalled the morning, "After we got through to safety and all and turned around, I saw five houses floating down the creek and you could walk on, from one to the other. One house particularly...at the time I didn't know who they were, but, I found out later, they was the Ballard and Janice Lou Carter family. They was five of them in the house...They're all gone."

The dam belonged to the Pittston Company, built to hold the waste-water by-products of their coal mining operations. A company official told reporters, "'We're investigating the damage which was caused by the flood, which we believe, of course, was an Act of God.' The dam was simply 'incapable of holding the water God poured into it.'"

Shirley Marcum saw it differently, "I didn't see God a-drivin them slate trucks up there and wearin' a hard-hulled cap. I didn't see that at no time when I visited the dam. That's the way I feel about it. I don't believe it was an 'Act of God,' it was an 'Act of Man.'"

Pittston knew twenty-four hours in advance that the water was reaching dangerous levels and that weather forecasts did not expect the rain to stop. The head of Pittston strip mining operations in that area, worried the dam wouldn't hold, contacted Steve Dasovitch, the general boss for Pittston in that area. Dasovitch "decided to reassure people downstream that nothing was going to happen...and was on his way out of the valley when the dam did go."

Organized through the West Virginia Black Lung Association, the people of West Virginia formed a Citizens' Commission to Investigate the Buffalo Creek Disaster. Of the official government account of the disaster Rev. Jim Somerville, Secretary of the Citizens' Commission said, "We were (sic.) suspicious of the report that takes so long to write, and has so many "ifs, ands, and buts" that it really says nothing." So the Citizens' Commission held public hearings, carefully studied the records released by public agencies, and published their own account.

According to Rev. Somerville, "the Citizens' Commission began to say quite early. 'We think that this coal company, Pittston, has murdered the people, and we call upon the prosecuting attorney and the judge in Logan County...to prosecute and bring to trial this coal company.'" Rev. Somerville also said, "One of the things that the Citizens' Commission found as it did its work on Buffalo Creek was that there was more to do on Buffalo Creek than merely find out the facts of the disaster. We felt that if we were a citizens' commission, then we could not be merely a fact-finding group but that, somehow, our membership on that Commission had to support the effort on that creek by people to do something about that disaster. We were trying to say to West Virginians that bodies of citizens need to bring the government to, uh, accountability."

Samuel Hickman, Executive Director of the National Association of Social Workers, West Virginia Chapter
Charleston, WV
Photo: Colleen Wessel-McCoy

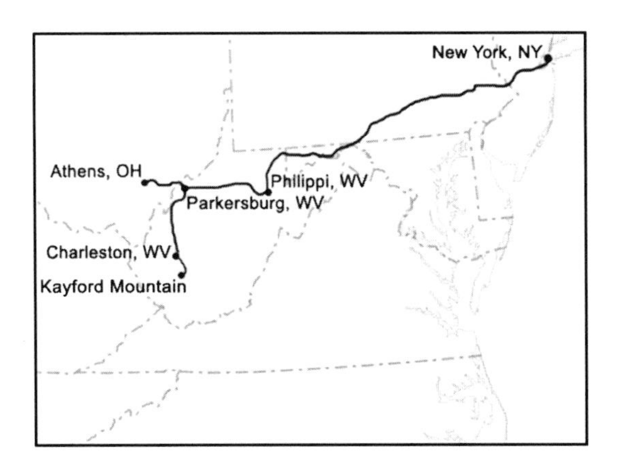

Friday, January 12

Chapter 7

Itinerary:

Biblical Reflection

Travel to Kayford Mountain, south of Charleston, WV, hosted by Julian Martin and Larry Gibson of the West Virginia Highland Conservancy

Travel to the Highlander Research and Education Center near New Market, Tennessee

Musical tribute to Paul Robeson performed by Derrick McQueen

Overnight at Workshop Center of the Highlander Research and Education Center

Selene Kaye (left), Sara Suman (right), and others prepare sandwiches for lunch later that day
Parkersburg, WV
Photo: Gayle Irvin

Larry Gibson (left) tells immersion participants about his fight to save his land from coal mining companies.
Kayford Mountain, WV
Photo: Adam Barnes

Drew Paton
Union Theological Seminary

Ground to Stand On

> "Go for a walk in the woods. Be real quiet and listen. The wilderness will talk to you. But I guarantee you – Come to see me and I'll put you on a mine site... and let you go for a walk. And nothing will talk to you." -Larry Gibson

Larry Gibson hears the roar of heavy machinery twenty-four hours a day, seven days a week. The 900 acres surrounding his small family plot on Kayford Mountain in Boone County, West Virginia, are owned by the Massey Energy Company, the fifth largest coal company in the United States. His great–great–grandfather Crockett Stanley settled on Kayford Mountain 186 years ago and more than 300 of his relatives are buried there. For the last twenty years Larry has endured this incessant noise. In an effort to scare him off his land his trailer has been vandalized, shot at, and flipped over. His dogs have been killed. His truck was pushed into a river. The area around his home is periodically showered with debris from the explosions at the nearby mine. Sink holes have developed in the family cemetery and carried off the remains of many of his loved ones. All of this while the noise of heavy machinery serves as a constant reminder that the setting for all his childhood memories, the mountains that he says give him life, the rivers that flow between them, and every living thing on them and in them is being destroyed.

The modern approach to mining, mountaintop removal—"peak reduction" mining, as the coal companies call it—allows the coal companies to remove as much as 700 feet from a mountain using explosives in order to get at the coal below. In Larry's words, "they used to take the coal from the mountain. Now they take the mountain from the coal." It will take 3,000 years for the ecosystem to restore itself when the mining is done and the mountains are gone forever. The land which Larry Gibson refuses to sell to the Massey Energy Company contains a quantity of coal currently valued at 4.5 million dollars, and they want him off it.

Two hundred yards from his front door there is a great, grey ulcer in the earth. We walked there together. Where mountains and lush forests once stood, there is only an enormous pit, several hundred feet deep—a desolate, lunar landscape whose only sign of life is the rumbling of heavy machinery. The land has been raped and murdered. The mutilation of the victim is continuous and ongoing. It is happening, even now, as I write these words and as you read them. It will happen until there is nothing left and then it will happen elsewhere.

Larry said to us, "if you're not going to do something about this, you're wasting my time!" And then, when we sang and cried together he said, "you folks... you really are going to do something, aren't you?" I hope and pray—I insist in the name of God that we live up to our reputation as members of the Union Theological Seminary community, to our heritage as people of faith, and to our responsibility as human beings and find a way to stand with Larry Gibson. Larry Gibson and the many thousands like him around the world—the impoverished and oppressed who stand up, who fight back—are the only hope we have. If we do not stand with them, this has all been for show—and catharsis is our only achievement. If we are to be of any use on this earth we must make their struggle our own.

> **Andrea Roske-Metcalfe**
>
> *Mountaintop Removal*
>
> As we were walking toward the mining site, I asked Larry to describe the difference between strip mining and mountain top removal. "Well," he began, "strip mining is where they take the coal from the mountain, and mountain top removal is where they take the mountain from the coal."
>
> Holy s***, I thought, as I stepped up to the edge of the ridge...he's absolutely right.

Mountaintop removal coal mining in process, viewed from the edge of Larry Gibson's property
Kayford Mountain, WV
Photo: Peter Cava

Ben Cherland at the edge
Kayford Mountain, WV
Photo: Colleen Wessel-McCoy

Alix Webb
Poverty Initiative

Gates of Hell

One member of our group asked our host Larry Gibson, "What is the difference between strip-mining for coal and Mountaintop Removal?" He said, "Well, I guess strip mining is about taking coal away from the mountain . . . and Mountaintop Removal is taking the mountain away from the coal."

The journey to witness this horror began on Larry Gibson's property; a rolling West Virginia mountain peak covered with hardwood trees. Larry and his family have lived on Kayford Mountain or the surrounding area for 185 years. The property used to cover 465 additional acres but they were signed away years ago for "a dollar and change per acre" by relatives who were unable to read.

Sign on Kayford Mountain
Photo: Erica Almiron, Media Mobilizing Project

Larry led us across his property to a place he calls the "Gates of Hell." Here I stood at the edge of what remained of his family's mountain. As I looked over I saw what the death of mountains looks like. I saw stripped, bare rock; blasted and bombed to expose the slim black veins of coal. According to Larry, some of the blasts are so violent that they will bend the nails backwards in his home on the peak. I saw three men in massive machines who in three years will turn this mountain into a pile of rock. I watched dump-trucks carry dusty gravel, down to a ragged, shelled out crevice, lift, and empty it in a small avalanche of shards.

It takes 3,000 years to create three inches of top soil. It takes top soil to grow trees and it takes trees to create top soil. Because there are now neither trees nor topsoil, the Gates of Hell have become an unrecognizable memory of a vast land, once green, once free, once tree-covered, once alive, now stripped, devoured, destroyed, so that nothing can grow there.

As I stood on the edge of Larry's property and stared at this destruction I had many thoughts. I thought of the passages of Ruth we have been reading this week. I thought about the choices she and Naomi had to make, the choices of women without. I thought of loosing a homeland.

I thought about the soup kitchen and food bank I visited on Wednesday where in the poorest district of Ohio, an area with 29% unemployment. Cars line up for a mile down the road starting as early as 4 a.m. to begin receiving boxes of food staples when the food bank opens at 8 a.m. Many days, this food bank location has 750 families pass through its food lines in just two hours. The workers here also make breakfast and lunch for 500 Head Start children every day and every Friday send hundreds of extra packets of food home with children who won't have enough food over the weekend. In short, here in this small area of the US, thousands of people are hungry.

I think of the time I spent with Candy Adams, a woman who lives on Chestnut Ridge, just outside Philippi, WV, a mixed-heritage woman, Native, African and white like all of "her kind" (as she calls her surrounding family). She told me about her mother dropping dead last

Mountaintop Removal coal mining in action
Kayford Mountain, WV
Photo: Selene Kaye

year at forty-two years old right in front of her eyes after she'd come to visit Candy in the Air Force. I drove with Candy through the hills and saw the land and the homes that her family has lived on and in for hundreds of years. I saw her favorite place in the forest and the river she "body-rafts" down every summer with her sons. I thought of who Candy was to this community: someone who herself struggled to find a job back in her home town after her tour in the Air Force and also someone who just that day while filling out surveys with members from our group at a low-income apartment project in Philippi, knew exactly what to do for a woman was in serious distress – drool hanging out of an alcoholic, epileptic mouth.

I thought of all the facts and stories, people and lives of this week. The lives and the land all being so efficiently disassembled beyond the edge of Larry's peak.

And I thought about something that has been bothering me for some time, something I have struggled with – the concept of evil. I fear the term. I am quick to anger at the way it is used lightly and with such terrible consequences when applied to ideas, people, children, and nations. I have wanted to fight people for using it when they apply it to these things. I have considered that I do not believe in it. But today, looking at the brutality of what has been done to this ravaged mountain, to a whole horizon of ancient land, I feel I have to reconsider all that I have thought.

I don't know another image that could hold and embrace all the things witnessed by each of us this week in this terribly abused region – Appalachia and of the growing poverty in this world that surrounds us daily. For me, it took something this enormous, the sacrifice of this mountain range, to hold all of these terrors and all of this grief and rage of millions of lives and millions of years. As I stood at Larry's gate and beheld it all I accepted that I may believe in and have witnessed evil in this world.

I also remembered a time earlier this week when I felt what some might call a moment of grace. Six of us: two from Appalachia, three from

Union, one from Columbia University School of Social Work, some brown, some white, some men, some women, all human, stood together deep in the hollers of a West Virginia ridge on a snow-covered bridge surrounded by the powerful, roaring sound of a rushing river. There was bright sun on the snow and a joy at being together in a most beautiful place. I felt the hope of coming to know one another and the possibility of hoping together.

I believe in the possibility of such moments supporting me to join a fight against evil. I leave this place thankful and thoughtful of the strength to stand at the Gates of Hell and to stand on the bridge and then to step forward.

Peter Cava surveys the damage
Kayford Mountain, WV
Photo: Justin Ward

Justin Ward
Union Theological Seminary

God on Location: A Theological Reflection on Mountaintop Removal

> "I have been to the mountaintop, but it wasn't there."
> –Bumper sticker on Larry Gibson's truck

On Friday, January 12th, we took an unexpected trip to the top of Kayford Mountain in Sharon, West Virginia. As soon as we piled out of our minivans, we were greeted by a man named Larry, who I suspect, is in his late fifties. Larry knows no home other than the one he has on this mountain, the land which his family has farmed for 186 years. Larry takes great pride in his home and the long-term romance his family has enjoyed with the mountain.

Eighteen years ago that romance suffered a devastating blow when coal miners bought up the land surrounding Larry's and began to ravage it through Mountaintop Removal, or MTR, a form of mining where coal miners literally chop off the tops of mountains in order to extract the coal from underneath them. Once the mountaintops have been destroyed and the coal has been removed, it is cleaned and sold to power plants that rely on coal as a source of fuel. Mining companies see the huge profits that come from these transactions, and seemingly none of the devastating, long-term effects that MTR and fossil-fuel burning have on our environment. The exact opposite is true for Larry and many others: despite the land's rich abundance of natural resources, the people of Appalachia remain some of the poorest in our country. In addition, it's Larry—not the miners—who must try to sleep at night while heavy machinery works around the clock to topple the mountaintops in his backyard.

Larry said he was speaking to us as though we might be the last group he ever sees. It's not an unlikely possibility for Larry. Since the mining company became his next door neighbor, Larry has been shot at repeatedly in determined efforts to get him off his land.

Larry realizes that he is living on top of a gold mine, but refuses to give up his home. A few years ago, the mining company offered him $150,000 for his land—a small fraction of the $450 million worth of coal that lies underneath his property. But in Larry's eyes, the mountain he lives on and the history it contains is priceless and not up for sale.

The back of Larry Gibson's truck
Photo: Selene Kaye

As we prepared to walk through the ridge to see the devastation of mountaintop removal for ourselves, Larry said, "Before we leave, I must tell you that what you are about to see is far worse than anything you ever could have imagined." He was right.

"Hell's Gate" is what Larry calls the line that divides his property and that which belongs to the mining company. It's an appropriate name, since the trees that once signified life on the mountains adjacent to Larry's property have been destroyed, never to grow again.

Where is God in all of this, you might ask? I've been asking that question myself a lot lately. Could it really be true that God doesn't care about the earth since Mountaintop Removal is permitted to take place in our country? After all, it's been eighteen years since mountaintop removal began in Larry's backyard. Why does Larry continue to pray and speak to groups like ours? Why doesn't he just give up?

I'd like to suggest that it's because God doesn't want him to. Theologian Sallie McFague imagines that the earth is God's body. If we imagine with her, we must consider that the tops being severed from mountains are not only destroying the land; they're leaving holes in the body of God. We must consider that in ravaging the land, we are ravaging our own Creator. Perhaps the passionate plea for help we hear from Larry is the voice of God welling up inside of him, provoking him to take a stand against injustice in the land, the body of God. Perhaps Mountaintop Removal is far more devastating to God than anyone else.

If the coal found inside mountains was meant for us to use, it surely doesn't seem that it should have to come at the cost of losing the mountains—but that's what is happening. And the mountains are not all we're losing. The recent United Nations report on global warming indicates that domestic and international dependency on coal and other fossil fuels for energy is to blame for the alarming rise in average temperatures across the globe. Overwhelming evidence suggests that if we continue to rely on coal and do not shift our energy dependency to renewable sources, like the sun, wind, and water, it seems likely that miners will have no choice but to continue destroying mountains. Temperatures will continue to rise. Rivers, lakes, and streams will eventually dry up. Dreaming for a white Christmas will have to remain simply that—a dream, a thing of the past. As I write this, it is February in New York City and so far this winter, the city has yet to see a significant snowfall. Though I do believe the earth needs people like Larry to speak on its behalf, I believe it's also finding ways to speak for itself. Does this mean we can no longer be trusted?

Coal is so close to the surface that it shows through anywhere there is even mild erosion.
Kayford Mountain, WV
Photo: Quan Blanche, Media Mobilizing Project

The same U.N. report also says that global warming is a "runaway train" that will take centuries to slow down. Does that mean that we should just sit back and watch it roll on by? I don't think so, nor do I think that's what God would have us to do. Christian environmentalist and professor Calvin Dewitt says, "Our task is to be faithful, not necessarily successful." He says that if we become faithful stewards in pursuing the integrity of the earth and integrity of society, it may become contagious.

Larry Gibson has caught the fever. I hope the rest of us can too.

Larry Gibson speaks from the edge
Kayford Mountain, WV
Photo: Peter Cava

Jessica Chadwick
Union Theological Seminary & Columbia University School of Social Work

Mountaintop Experiences: A sermon based on Exodus 3:1-6 and Luke 9:28-36

Moses stood on Mt Horeb, the mountain of God just beyond the wilderness, and suddenly the Lord appeared through a burning bush.

I'm sorry, but that just seems ridiculous. The God of the universe. God of Abraham, Isaac and Jacob, would appear through a blazing bush? A bush, blazing with flames and yet not burning? I would find it hard to believe. But Moses immediately recognized that he was in the presence of God and he knew that he was on Holy Ground. Suddenly, that piece of mountain, just beyond the wilderness, became the catalyst for the exodus of the Israelites out of slavery. For Moses it had been just an ordinary day, out attending to his flock—a shepherd looking for a place for his sheep to graze. It was an ordinary day in the life of an ordinary man. And then God showed up. And when God shows up, amazing things happen.

Later in the story, God instructs Moses to lead the Israelites out of the land of Egypt and into the promised land. Moses is to tell the people that "I AM" sent him and God assures Moses that the people will follow him. The Israelite slaves will be led by Moses through the wilderness and into the promised land.

It is interesting that this mountain, the mount of Horeb, the mountain of God, is surrounded in this story by wilderness. Moses is wandering with his flock through the wilderness toward this mountain when God is revealed to him. Moses is transformed and is given the tall order of obeying God to secure the liberation of the Israelite people. And then he spends the next forty years of his life wandering through the wilderness again.

The story of the Transfiguration, as told by Luke, is much the same. Jesus and the disciples were journeying through the countryside near Bethsaida. There were crowds of people following Jesus wanting to watch the healer and miracle-performer. The disciples had been on journeys like this with Jesus many times before; it was an ordinary experience. A week later Jesus takes the disciples to the top of the mountain to pray. They had an intense religious experience in which Jesus' face turns dazzling white and God is revealed through a cloud. And we can read later in that chapter in Luke, that the disciples, later that day, were unable to perform a healing on a boy and Jesus was disappointed. Their mountaintop experience was over and they were back in the wilderness.

In Scripture, the symbol of the wilderness refers to places in which people may fast and practice discernment, like Jesus and John the Baptist. Or where people spend time wandering through their daily lives, waiting for their liberation, as in the exodus of the Israelites. The wilderness is the ordinary experience of our lives. The place where we wait, where we exist and where we live in the in between, in the valleys. The places that are not the mountaintops.

I had the opportunity to go to the mountaintop during the Union journey through Appalachia. Like Moses' experience at Mt. Horeb and like the disciples experience at the Transfiguration, our trip to the mountain was an unexpected occurence. We were in the wilderness and God showed up and we had a mountaintop experience. I'd like to tell you a little about what happened.

I thought I had planned our trip to the minute. I knew where we were going when, who was driving, how we were getting there, what we would see when we got there, how long it would take, and when people could stop to use the restroom. But something unexpected happened. Though the idea had terrified me, we had left our schedule open on

Friday morning in case we found anything exciting that we wanted to do along the way. My co-workers never gave me a satisfying justification for this gaping hole in our itinerary, but as they were veteran trip planners, I went with it. And it turns out they were right. On Thursday afternoon we were meeting with the Direct Action Welfare Group and the West Virginia Council of Churches. Someone in our group mentioned wanting to learn more about coal mining in the region. At the same time every West Virginia native in the room said that we must go to the mountain to see Larry. Fortunately, we had a slot we could fit him in.

Early on Friday morning we caravanned our five mini-vans and three cars through the mountain terrain of West Virginia. When the two lane road turned into a one lane road, which turned into muddy gravel, we kept driving another twenty minutes up the side of a mountain and at the top of it, we met Larry. He told us about his family living on Kayford mountain for 186 years. Recently a coal company bought up the land around his mountain to begin mountaintop removal mining. When asked to explain how this type of mining was different from underground mining and strip mining Larry replied, "Strip mining is when you take the coal from the mountain. Mountain top removal is when you take the mountain from the coal." Because Larry has refused to sell his land, it is possible to stand at the top of his mountain and look to the site of the Mountaintop Removal all around him.

Caravaning up Kayford Mountain
Photo: Colleen Wessel-McCoy

We hiked up Kayford mountain about half a mile. We saw signs to the right and the left warning us to watch out for falling rock. One sign instructed us to the number of whistle blasts that can be heard before they blow a piece of mountain off with dynamite. I don't think any of us were prepared for what we would see just beyond what Larry called "The Gates of Hell."

The earth movers used for Moutaintop Removal are gigantic, even making a big truck look small in comparison.
Kayford Mountain, WV
Photo: Sara Smith, Media Mobilizing Project

We stepped to the edge of Kayford mountain and saw complete nothingness. In Mountaintop Removal mining, the coal company blows up the top of the mountain, and removes the coal there, then blows up more of the mountain, and removes the coal there. This is done until the mountain is leveled out. It is difficult to distinguish where the mountain once was and where the valley once was. Rocks from the blasts are dumped into any close-by holler. The explosions have spewed rocks the size of cars onto his property.

The coal company employs forty-five people in three shifts of fifteen people each for twenty-four hours a day. There is a constant low rumble of machinery in the background. This is interrupted by occasional explosive blasts. We heard Larry talk about how the coal company has tried to get him to leave by threatening him, shooting at him, and killing his dog. In all, Larry has documented 109 counts of violence against him.

Many of us were moved to tears by Larry's account of how for twenty years he has asked the county to get electricity up to his mountain so that his family could have running water, the county denying every request. But when the coal company moved in, they were granted rights to electricity so that they could operate twenty-four hours a day. We were moved when we heard Larry talk about playing in the forests of these mountains as a boy. He told us that before, he could have given one of us a pocket knife and we would have been able to live on his property and survive. However, now, at this mining site, nothing will ever grow again. Life has been stripped from the land.

We were encouraged by Larry's strength. He has taken a stand for his family and his land and he has motivated others to fight against the exploitation of the Appalachian peoples.

We stayed at the Gates of Hell for a long time. I was one of the last ones to leave. I looked over the edge of Kayford mountain at the nothingness that existed below. I watched the machines go back and forth digging coal and dumping what they couldn't sell off the side. I thought about the men working for the coal company driving these dump trucks and wondered what it feels like to destroy creation in order to earn a living. I remembered the peaceful, spiritual, and playful times that I have had in the mountains when I lived in West Virginia. I was torn apart. For me this was no mountaintop experience; I was watching the mountain being taken away.

But that is exactly when God showed up. Our group of forty-seven somberly walked down from the Gates of Hell back to the gravel parking lot beneath Larry's house. Unable to find words to respond, we sang with him. We didn't know what else to do. We were so moved by Larry's strength to stand up against injustices that we wanted to show our support. And there on his mountain, with the rumbling of machinery and explosives in the background, we sang, "We shall not be moved. Just like a tree that's planted by the water, we shall not be moved." In that moment, when we were in the valley of despair, broken and feeling destroyed, God was revealed and we were transformed.

Moses, Jesus and the disciples, Larry and us, we had mountaintop experiences--experiences of transformation--where God showed up at an unexpected time and in an unexpected way: in a blazing bush, in a cloud, in a song.

These are the experiences where God's revelation is so close and so real that one's spirituality is elevated to a level beyond human comprehension. And it doesn't just happen on mountains. We've all had experiences like that in our lives at retreats, or time with family, or personal devotion time, or fellowship time at this church. Times when we feel so close to God that our hearts feel complete and we can imagine no other way of living. These are the times when, like Moses, we have wandered through the wilderness, like the disciples we have endured the ridicule of the crowds, and like Larry we have stood our ground against the powerful. These are the times God has helped us make it to the other side—to that bush, that cloud, that song—that place of being on the top of that mountain that is so close to God that our spirits feel like one. To that place of Holy Ground where we must take off our shoes to walk.

The question I've had to ask myself is what do I do when I have to leave that mountain? The mountaintop experience, an elevated and complete spirituality, is not where we live our daily lives. It is the extraordinary place, contrasted to the wilderness of ordinary life. But it is in the ordinary places that we do the work God has called us to do.

When Moses came down from the mountain he had to lead people through the desert for forty years. When Jesus came down from the mountain he was confronted with people who needed healing. And our class is trying to figure out how we will respond to injustices in Appalachia and at home.

Larry told us when we first met him that if we came to see the Gates of Hell and heard his story and then did nothing about it, that we were wasting his time. Hours later, after we sang with Larry, he said, through tears, "Now I know you will do something."

We all have to come down from the mountaintop experience. It is the way of life. We must continue to live through the wilderness, the unfaithfulness, and the struggle. What counts is what we do when we get off the mountain .

Moses led his people to liberation. His experience at Mount Horeb was transformative not only for his own relationship with God, but for all the Israelites. This mountaintop experience was mixed with journeys through the wilderness and through the desert and ended in the liberation of the people of God. What began in the wilderness was highlighted by a brief transformative moment followed by forty years of living in the wilderness until liberation occurred.

Jesus and the disciples came down from the mountain and the persecution of Jesus began. The trials and accusations that led to Jesus's death and resurrection, and ultimately to our salvation, happened after this transformative experience on the top of this mountain.

(top left to right) Gayle Irvin, Stefanie Schoen, Tallu Schuyler, John Wessel-McCoy, Liz Theoharis, (front left to right) Jessica Pullido, Sara Suman, Larry Gibson, and Erica Almiron
Kayford Mountain, WV
Photo: Selene Kaye

And so it is with our immersion experience. The Poverty Initiative seeks to build a social movement, led by the poor, to end poverty. It is a process of journeys through the valleys and the mountains. It could take forty years or more in the wilderness, but hopefully less, before the impoverished peoples in this world are liberated from their oppression. And that is what we will do now that we are down from this mountain. We are committed to continue to tell Larry's story and the story of others in the Appalachian region who are being displaced and exploited and who have chosen to stand against injustice in the world. We are committed to continue to build relationships with the heroes and the prophets we met on our trip.

In April we will hold a Truth Commission where we will invite Larry and others to come to Union Theological Seminary to tell their stories of living in impoverished circumstances and the work they have done to overcome those situations. We will support Larry when he goes before the United Nations to testify to the consequences of Mountaintop Removal mining. And, because of this trip and the impoverishment that I saw and have seen before, I have committed my life to work with the poor, perhaps one day in West Virginia.

But I want to ask you, what will you do? What will happen when your mountaintop experience has ended, when that time when you felt so close to God has stopped and you find yourself back in the valley of your life? Or perhaps you are living in the wilderness now, experiencing the ordinary of life? How will use your transformative mountaintop experience to lead others to liberation or salvation?

Each of us has had mountaintop experiences and we have had to come down from the mountain. Some of us, like Larry, have even seen those very mountains blasted apart bit by bit. We still have to come down from the mountain and live in the valleys or the wilderness. But we have the hope of transformation and the knowledge that God shows up in unexpected ways and in unexpected places: in a blazing bush, in a cloud, in a song. God will show up on our mountain or in our valley.

And when God shows up, amazing things happen.

The writer of Psalm 11 asks, "When the foundations are crumbling, what will the righteous do?" We must continue the work of liberation, of salvation, of support, so that we did not just waste Larry's time or our time at the top of that mountain, but so that we may be continually transformed and be transforming others toward a right relationship with our Creator God.

Larry Gibson
Kayford Mountain, WV
Photo: Katy Moore

Looking over the edge.
Kayford Mountain, WV
Photo: Adam Barnes

Home on Kayford Mountain
Photo: Sarah Smith, Media Mobilizing Project

Katy Moore
Union Theological Seminary

Gentrification in Appalachia?

I'm a city kid. When I think about poverty, that's the kind I mean. And I'm part of that young, queer, artsy population that's always the first step in gentrification—we find our affordable, "quirky" housing in low-income neighborhoods, and then our white faces make it safe for developers to buy up property, driving out the long-time residents. Which, of course, I hate. Beyond the fact of rising rents forcing me out in turn, I can't stand seeing the destruction of my adopted neighborhood. This vibrant community is being ripped apart at the seams, patched with Starbucks and vague, lifeless brushed steel—and I am complicit.

So, reducing our social impact has become a huge topic of conversation among my friends. How can we alleviate what feels like an inevitable consequence of being white and broke? When I was planning for the Poverty Initiative's trip, the word "gentrification" came up as it usually does, and I joked that I didn't think it was going to be a huge issue in West Virginia. Rural poverty is a result of too little economic investment, not too much, right?

(Parenthetically, it turns out that the eastern panhandle of West Virginia (where we didn't visit) is going through something very much like urban gentrification. Folks who work in DC have been moving further and further out, in search of lower rents, and the low cost of living in West Virginia is apparently worth the hassle and the gasoline consumption of a two-hour commute into the city. In turn, commercial development and fancy new housing complexes are booming in these areas to serve the new, presumably moneyed, population. Just as this pattern of development is the norm in every major city these days, it seems like it's spreading further out into many previously-rural areas.)

As expected, what I knew of as "gentrification"—new, $1.5 million condos springing up in poorer neighborhoods—wasn't the issue in the parts of Appalachia we traveled in. The poverty I saw for the bulk of the trip was a result of all the local industries having disappeared. When those jobs are replaced, to some small degree, it is by corporations like Wal-Mart. The coal companies got rich at the expense of West Virginia's citizens and resources, but at the same time, they did provide employment (and, occasionally, some measure of security) for a huge percentage of the population. Now that they're gone, mechanized, and/or have replaced the local labor force with their own people, not much is left except multinationals like Wal-Mart.

West Virginia mountain landscape after mountaintop removal coal mining
Photo: Sarah Smith, Media Mobilizing Project

This sprawling symbol of the demise of local business, boycotted by good liberals the world over—those who can afford to, at least—this is the largest employer in West Virginia. Much like the miners who were paid with vouchers that could only be spent at the company store, their poverty-level wages mean that suddenly, Wal-Mart's "discount" prices are all the workers can afford. So, yes, perhaps Wal-Mart is bringing jobs to West Virginia. But on the other hand, any money they might bring to the area goes right back into the company coffers because their employees have no choice but to support their own wealthy employers.

In the end, though, the state of West Virginia has little choice but to welcome coal mines and Wal-Marts; these are the only companies willing to invest in a region with such little economic power. As is often the case with investors seen as essential to a region's economy, the state government seems to be willing to give these companies anything they want, to the point of draining any of the land's natural resources. Even when lawmakers see the destruction being wrought, they are scared silent by the prospect of upsetting the company that is their county's only economic base, or they are outvoted by their peers who are.

Stanley Heirs Park sign
Kayford Mountain, WV
Photo: Colleen Wessel-McCoy

At the end of the week, we paid an unplanned visit to Larry Gibson and Kayford Mountain, where his family has lived for over 186 years. He took us up to what he called the "Gates of Hell"—a Mountaintop Removal site eating away at his beloved mountain. These gorgeous mountains, which in summer are covered with a lush carpet of trees, fluffy greens of every possible shade and more; these mountains that have sustained generations of families like Larry's; these mountains where no matter how poor you are, some food will grow for you; these mountains are being reduced to desolate, gray piles of gravel, where nothing can grow. The only life that's found on one of these sites is encased in steel—a handful of machine operators, each hidden away inside an enormous yellow piece of de-struction equipment.

This wasn't my first visit to a Mountaintop Removal site. In 2001, the summer after I finished high school, my church youth group went on a mission trip to the Kanawha Valley of West Virginia (also home to Kayford Mountain), which has been ravaged by strip mining for decades before Mountaintop Removal took over where it left off. We spent the week repairing homes in the community, many of which had been devastated by the floods and landslides that are the results of such extensive mining. While it was a valuable experience—seeing the destruction wreaked by coal mining on individual families was a shocking first look at rural poverty—we didn't talk about any of the reasons that such poverty exists, or even challenge the idea that poverty should exist in the first place.

We had Wednesday afternoon free to spend as a youth group. While other church groups found public pools, went to the movies, or relaxed in some other way, our pastor decided, for reasons he never explained to us, that we should visit one of the coal mines to which so much of that area has been subjected. So without any introduction beyond "we're going to a coal mine," we sat through a video and a lecture on the "revolutionary new mining practices" we were going to see, both produced by the coal company. I wish I could see those now, knowing what I do about the social and environmental effects of these practices, but at the time we were a bunch of bored high school kids sitting through a presentation on something none of us knew anything about or really had any interest in.

We spent the rest of the afternoon driving, in our minivans, around on the winding roads cut through the giant piles of rock. Afterwards, there was a general consensus that this was a terrible way to spend an afternoon, but there was really no discussion of why we felt that way. Thinking back, I remember feeling (in addition to boredom) like we were wandering around some kind of desert wasteland. I knew that coal mines were supposed to have lots of people working in them, but I didn't see a soul. I assumed maybe they weren't working that day. Nothing much seemed to be happening in this surreal, lunar landscape—gray and dusty as far as I could see, interrupted only by occasional yellow machines with 9-foot tires. It was dead, silent, vacant, and I wanted nothing more than to be out of there, back out into the lush green mountainscape I was already coming to love so much.

On top of Kayford Mountain, with Larry, we walked half a mile or so on his property before we got to Hell's Gate. Though I was in a group of 50-some people, I felt such peace and calm, being on top of that mountain in its natural state. The quiet beauty of the mountain settled around me, and the non-stop motion of the week was briefly forgotten. In that short walk, I realized why all those Biblical writers considered mountaintops to be sacred spaces, where one can be closer to God. There is something special, liminal, something not-quite-definable about a mountaintop.

Our path led us across the literal gate, the property line, and then the earth fell away. It was a bite out of the land, a sudden ragged ending to the soft mountain on which I stood. Where the greens and reds and browns of the mountain should have been, there was just gray. Acres and acres of gray nothingness. As I contemplated the deathscape laid out before me, the only word that made sense was "rape." I was looking at the bloody, eviscerated vagina of America, where capitalism has left West Virginia lying out to die.

Climbing up to the edge of Larry Gibson's property.
Kayford Mountain, WV
Photo: Colleen Wessel-McCoy

I had to step back. I had to put a camera between me and this vision of my own bleeding body. I stood in the epicenter of the systemic exploitation that is corporate greed, cutting its wide swath on the earth and its people. The black dust I saw, in a few scattered stripes, was the prize, the price tag put on God's body, the earth. I saw "Everyday Low Prices," I saw luxury condos, I saw New England grocery store aisles full of papayas and mangos in January, I saw all the amenities I have been taught that I deserve. This, there on the mountain, is the price I pay daily; if the destruction I saw is what it takes to power a coal plant, then the energy I consume for my transportation, my eating habits, my laptop—my lifestyle is making that coal mine necessary.

Suddenly, gentrification was the issue again. Disguised in a different form, certainly, but what I saw on that mountain was Larry Gibson's family chased out for coal, for profits, with no regard for where they will go or how they will live when their land has been chewed up and spit out into the valley. I might as well have been watching the African-American families of Harlem being driven out for the Lenox Grand condominiums, or the Dominican and Puerto Rican families of Providence's West Side pushed aside for Rising Sun Mills. The message is the same, the disrespect is the same.

No people, no culture, no homeland is worth as much as profit. The exploitation crosses divisions of race, language, or region: wherever people with less money own or possess something that people with more money want, the result is the same. Nothing can stand in the way of The Market, and as we continue to focus singlemindedly on Progress and Wealth and Energy, countless millions are evicted, literally and symbolically, and left to die by the wayside, having been stripped of land, culture, and dignity.

Larry Gibson surveys the
Mountaintop Removal
coalmining adjacent to his
family's property
Kayford Mountain, WV
Photo: Colleen Wessel-McCoy

The Appalachian Coalfields Delegation to the United Nations
Submitted by Colleen Wessel-McCoy

Antrim Caskey hosts "The War in Appalachia" (www.clipfile.org/antrim), a website that documents the affects of coal mining on life—human and nonhuman—in Appalachia and the fight those affected by it wage to change the situation. On May 6, 2006 he posted this entry, which includes Larry Gibson who spoke to us at his home on Kayford Mountain, WV during our immersion:

> Members of the Appalachian Coalfields Delegation to the United Nations listen to Edwin Pinero, a federal environmental executive defend the concept of clean coal, May 5, 2006.
>
> Coalfield delegates claim coal is killing them and the land their families have inhabited for up to two hundred years. Pictured here from right, West Virginia Delegates: Donnetta Blankenship, Mingo County; Larry Gibson, Kayford Mountain; Maria Gunnoe, Bob White, WV; and Pam Maggard, Perry County, KY.
>
> A youth delegation also participated, expressing their concern for a commitment to renewable, sustainable energy.
>
> The Appalachian Delegation is made of ten residents of the coalfields of West Virginia and Kentucky, who have come to the UN to explain how their lives, in the hollows of the Appalachian mountains are being destroyed by irresponsible and destructive coal mining. UNCSD will continue its annual session through May 12, 2006.

Photo credit: Antrim Caskey/WorldPictureNews

Colleen Wessel-McCoy
Union Theological Seminary

Strength in the Wilderness

God *is* where people struggle for their full humanity—this is what I learned in Professor Brigitte Kahl's *Biblical Exegesis* course (Fall 2006) where we spent time with the strange first verses of the third chapter of Luke:

> In the fifteenth year of the reign of Emperor Tiberius, when Pontius Pilate was governor of Judea, and Herod was ruler of Galilee, and his brother Philip ruler of the region of Ituraea and Trachonitis, and Lysanias ruler of Abilene, during the high priesthood of Annas and Caiaphas, the word of God came to John son of Zechariah in the wilderness. He went into all the region around the Jordan, proclaiming a baptism of repentance for the forgiveness of sins, as it is written in the book of the words of the prophet Isaiah,
>
> "The voice of one crying out in the wilderness:
> Prepare the way of the Lord, make his paths straight.
> Every valley shall be filled, and every mountain and hill shall be made low,
> and the crooked shall be made straight, and the rough ways made smooth;
> and all flesh shall see the salvation of God."

Those who were high are brought low, those who are low are brought up, and the consequence of this equality is *all* seeing the salvation of God.[1] This is the way Luke explains repentance, and upon close inspec-

[1] The final outcome, all flesh seeing the salvation of God, is at a particular (though unspecified) future moment: *ophetai* ("will see") is the future indicative form of *horao* ("to see"). But the occurrence of the transformation is ongoing. *Hetoimasate* ("prepare") and *roieite* ("make") are imperative verbs, which "implies that the action called for is to be prolonged or repeated" (Croy,

tion it is clear that he is not only speaking of spiritual change; reconciliation and liberation are tied together. In the first verses he identifies the current positions of power—the emperor, the governor, the local rulers and the temple priests, all people in high places who carry out the mechanics of empire, thereby benefiting from the oppression of people in low places—and then says that God is elsewhere, namely with John the Baptist in the wilderness.

Larry Gibson (left) explains his fight for justice to (left to right) Judith Scott, Stefanie Schoen, Joe Strife, Ellie Martin Cliffe and others Kayford Mountain, WV
Photo: Erica Almiron, Media Mobilizing Project

Wildernesses—uncontrolled places—are threatening to empires, because empires depend on control to maintain power. As regions with limited administrative control, wildernesses were historically where people oppressed by an empire exerted more autonomy.[2] Consequently they often served as the launching ground for insurgency and revolution. In Luke, God is with John in the wilderness—the place beyond the control of the empire and out of which the ways of empire are threatened. The baptism of repentance of which John speaks is coupled with a transformation to active participation in the powerful being made low and the powerless being brought up. This is the Lord's way.

A Primer of Biblical Greek, 158). The directions given by the text, "prepare the way" and "make paths straight" call for participation in the action of the text and are not limited to a particular time. It's not that human completion of a task (such as confession) will launch divine action in which humans play a passive role, but that humans participate in the transformation. Repentance must then be understood as both the change of mind and the consequential participation in the transformation of time and place.

[2] As in Exodus, the wilderness is the place where those who were once enslaved are now free.

To describe the audacity and spectacle of this transformation, to show how much God's way is in stark contrast to the imperial way, Isaiah and Luke employ a seemingly preposterous visual image: mountains being made low and valleys being filled. Seeing mountains being made low and valleys being filled from the precipice of Kayford Mountain, I could barely believe my eyes. I struggled to comprehend it. Mountaintop Removal coal mining is a total disruption of what seems inevitable and insurmountable.

Mountains made low
Kayford Mountain, WV
Photo: Peter Cava

It is morbidly ironic that coal companies are using their economic and political power to make mountains low. From positions of power (akin to the positions of power where God is not found in Luke 3.1-6), coal companies and government officials beholden to coal profits literally level mountains. Far from the way of God in which we are called to participate, this leveling is consistent with the way of empires past and present—the extraction of life from a land and from the people who call the land home. God's way is not the way of empire.[3]

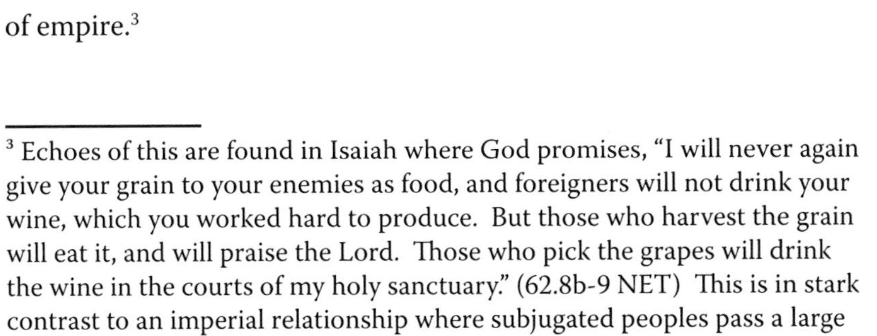

[3] Echoes of this are found in Isaiah where God promises, "I will never again give your grain to your enemies as food, and foreigners will not drink your wine, which you worked hard to produce. But those who harvest the grain will eat it, and will praise the Lord. Those who pick the grapes will drink the wine in the courts of my holy sanctuary." (62.8b-9 NET) This is in stark contrast to an imperial relationship where subjugated peoples pass a large portion (sometimes a majority) of their yield up to the subjugator. In God's time, needs are met by systemic fairness.

But during our travel we also met the voices in the wilderness—leaders from DAWG, Picture the Homeless and the Appalachian Coalfields Delegation to the United Nations. The wilderness out of which these leaders speak is not one of isolation and hopelessness, but a wilderness that threatens the ways of empire with organized resistance.[4]

Luke continues five verses later with John the Baptist explaining how those with power—tax collectors, people with wealth and imperial soldiers—might also participate in the transformation from the way of empire to the way of God. For the wealthy, "the person who has two tunics must share with the person who has none, and the person who has food must do likewise" (Luke 3.11b).[5] Tax collectors should collect no more than required (3.12). In other words, they should cease using their power as agents of the Roman Empire to financially exploit those they have power over by charging a higher tax rate and pocketing the difference. Likewise, soldiers of the Roman Empire are not to use their power to exploit or abuse people (3.13), which would have been a common practice in an occupied territory.

These are all ways of participating in justice, leveling the playing fields. Those who benefit from relationships of inequality must divest themselves of that power to exploit. They must surrender their own privilege. They must identify with the people rather than with the empire. Their freedom can no longer depend on the slavery of others. This is no easy task. Accustomed to the privileges of power, oppressors subjectively experience the liberation of the poor as the denial of their freedom,[6] so it rarely—perhaps never—happens without great force. But the gospel

[4] While in the past I had interpreted Isaiah's one voice in the wilderness as an isolated individual the world could not hear, the Appalachia immersion has helped me understand this text in a new light.

[5] This is reminiscent of Exodus, where manna is provided for all according to need, but attempts to store up extra manna beyond what is needed for the day are always defeated. The surplus manna spoils, and yet there is always enough manna the next day.

[6] That slave owners expected monetary compensation for the emancipation of their human 'property' is a relevant historical example.

asks for no less.

The Bible frequently draws a distinction between old and new ways, between old and new ages, and between old and new kingdoms, and it repeatedly demonstrates that the new age and new way is in the struggle of the oppressed. In the United States and in the world today, the new way, God's way, includes the abolition of poverty, led by the poor, who find their strength in the wilderness.

Larry Gibson (right) Sarah Suman (center) and Jan Rehmann (left)
Kayford Mountain, WV
Photo: Colleen Wessel-McCoy

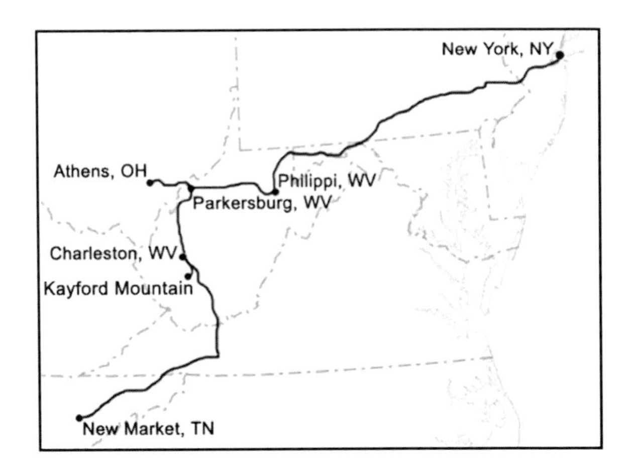

Saturday, January 13

Chapter 8

Itinerary:

Biblical Reflection

Music with Guy and Candy Carawan and an introduction to Highlander Research and Education Center by Susan Williams

Time for personal reflection, relaxation and exploring Highlander's Harry Lasker Memorial Library and Resource Center

Some gathered for a Truth Commission planning meeting

Liz Theoharis and Willie Baptist lead a conversation on "What is a Social Movement?"

Group reflection and closing

Bonfire and disco

Jan Rehmann reading on the lawn of the Highlander Research and Education Center
New Market, TN
Photo: Alix Webb

Liz Theoharis and Drew Paton on the porch of the Workshop Center at the Highlander Research and Education Center
New Market, TN
Photo: Jessica Chadwick

Workshop Cente
Highlander Research and Education Cente
New Market, T
Photo: Colleen Wessel-McCo

(above) Kumiko Kawasaki and (below) Tallu Schuyler
Highlander Research and Education Center
Photos: Sarah Smith, Media Mobilizing Project

Truth Commission planning meeting
Highlander Research and Education Cente
Photo: Jessica Chadwick

Ellie Martin Cliffe
Union Theological Seminary

God Is Here

A very dear person reminded me today that even though our experiences throughout this journey have exposed great struggle and injustice in Appalachia, God is here. In some places it was difficult to believe, especially as we watched people mutilating the earth at the mountaintop removal site. Considering ecotheologian Sallie McFague's assertion that the earth is the divine body, doesn't this mean that by damaging and abusing the earth (the land and its people), we are hurting God most of all?

Bonfire on the last night
Highlander Research and Education Center
Photo: Adam Barnes

At the same time, I can't think of anyone I've talked to who doesn't have hope that something positive is going to come of this. People are noticing commonalities in their struggles (related to poverty, education, other human rights, and the environment). My hope is that eventually, maybe soon, the eyes and ears of those in power will be opened and they will finally see, listen, and act.

Myles Horton, the man who founded the Highlander Center, wrote that our anger and drive need to be smoldering—not burning; flames go out faster. This movement is smoldering, and everything we've experienced on this trip has in some way contributed more fuel for it to continue.

Immersion participants gathered for biblical reflection in the main meeting room
Highlander Research and Education Center
New Market, TN
Photo: Colleen Wessel-McCoy

Liz Theoharis and Willie Baptist

What is a Social Movement?

Talk given at the Highlander Center on January 13, 2006, transcribed by Mica Root

Liz Theoharis: I think it's really appropriate that we're in this space here, and I want to talk a little bit about the connection between this space and the space at Union Theological Seminary, or at least the roots of the Poverty Initiative. I think folks that have done the assigned reading know that Myles Horton—and some other folks actually that were the founders of the Highlander Folk School back in the 1930s—were students at Union Theological Seminary, when they came up with the idea of how do they return back to the community that they came from and try to address some of the problems that they knew existed there. And they did a lot of thinking and a lot of talking and came up with this kind of model of a folk school. What would it be to bring Appalachian people together to learn from each other and study with each other and try to figure out a resolution to some of the problems that people were facing. So what they did was they traveled around while they were still in school and looked at different models—sounds a little familiar—and then they went and they talked to some prominent people, folks like Reinhold Niebuhr, who was one of the best known ethicists of this past generation and was a professor at Union Theological Seminary. And he ended up writing the first fundraising letter for what would become the Highlander Folk School. And to me that sounds a little familiar, because maybe folks don't know this but we've had to raise every bit of the money of the Poverty Initiative since its inception three years ago, and well, the first person we asked to write a fundraising letter for the Poverty Initiative was someone by the name of William Sloane Coffin, who was, I would say, the equivalent of my generation to who Reinhold Niebuhr was to that generation, a very prominent social justice leader and leader and pastor and chaplain who was the first religious leader to resist the Vietnam War and continued with social justice work, and actually was at Riverside Church, for folks up in the Columbia University area. And so I think that the story of the founding of Highlander and the start of the Poverty Initiative, and the founding and the continuation of Highlander and what we've been doing on this trip actually really resonate with each other.

And I think we want to take a couple of minutes now to think about the connection between the movements that Highlander was a part of and the movement that we're trying to be a part of and trying to commit to and trying to help to start, right now in the 21st century. For folks that have read this book, The Long Haul, or maybe studied the Civil Rights Movement, or the union and labor movement, some of these stories are going to be familiar; but I know that, growing up, I always heard the story of Rosa Parks, and I thought she was an old woman who got too tired and decided not to give up her seat. And it was random, and it was spontaneous, and oh my gosh look at that—then all of a sudden thousands of people stopped taking the bus the next day. And so then that's how I thought social change happened: it was random, and it was spontaneous, and it was people as just random individuals getting too tired, and then some other people joined, and that's how change happened. And I think change does happen that way—I don't want to say it doesn't—but it really was amazing for me to then study that Rosa Parks was the secretary of the NAACP, and she was a part of a bunch of women's groups in the Montgomery Area, who had actually been trying to have a bus boycott for some years before she got tired one day. And maybe most importantly at least to my thinking was the story that Rosa Parks had actually been at a human rights desegregation training at the Highlander Center just months before she got too tired. And so I think that one of the ways that I've been challenged in my life is I always think I am not Rosa Parks and I always think I am not Martin Luther King, and I am not all these different people, because I just am tired, or I have other commitments, or I need a lot of time to study or something. And what's been amazing about studying Rosa Parks and studying this Highlander Center has been to see the role that every individual has played, and the people that came around them to support them, to become the leaders that we now know. And I think we want to think about that a little bit too. Have we, in the last couple of days, met some of those people that are the next Rosa Parks, the next Fannie Lou Hamer, the next Chris Evans from the United Mine Workers? And how do we figure that out, and what is it to put those people into relationship, and what is it that a movement really is?

Willie's taught me a lot about movements and often says that for people of my generation—and I think this is so true—it's hard to know what a movement is, because I haven't lived through one. And so I do actually want to turn it over to Willie and have us hear a little bit about what is a social movement so that we can then be thinking about how to make those kinds of connections in terms of the work that we've been doing for this past week.

Willie Baptist: What keeps reverberating and keeps coming back in my mind is the comment from Larry, who says, "If you ain't gonna do nothing about what I've said, don't waste my time." And he says, "Excuse me, it might sound very harsh for me to say it this way," but he was reflecting on the deaths, the countless deaths and harshness of this society that is visiting increasing segments of men, women, and children of this society on a world, international scale. The urgency of the moment has to challenge each one of us in terms of what are our real commitments? Who are we? What are we about? What are the priceless things that we're prepared to die for so we have something to live for? These are the questions that all of us have to come to terms with. Larry posed it very eloquently and he posed it in a way that I'm going to constantly have to hear, at the moments when I retreat to my own individual self and get a bit selfish and get a bit trivial, when the life situation of this country and of the world are becoming more and more urgent in terms of us, on our watch, taking a stand and doing what he did. Clearly the issue that he spoke to, the front of struggle that he's involved in, is one of the many fronts of struggles that we experienced on this trip, but also there's still countless other fronts of struggles that are beginning to erupt throughout this country, where leaders like Larry are emerging, and leaders like ourselves are having to encounter and make decisions about. What is it that we're going to do to make a contribution? The things that are occurring, the deaths that are occurring as a result of the mass economic and social dislocations that are occurring in this country, are happening on our watch. The question is, what are we going to do about it?

And so these are the challenges that we have, and these are the challenges of a social movement. A social movement in my recollection, in my study of history, is a movement that is sustained by those who are committed, that are clear and competent and bring their own particular strength and bring their leadership capacities to the struggle. I might not be the kind of leader that Tallu could be; I might not be able to sing as well as she can sing; I might not have those kinds of strengths. But I can give what I can give, and each one of you can give what you can give in this process. So commitment, and the art of leadership, and the style and type of leadership, are all part of what a movement is about, especially in establishing that movement. It's very difficult to commit to something if you don't know what you're committing to. So there are a lot of people throwing around the term "movement," and they don't really know what a movement is. There's no way that they can know, because their experience is not telling them that, and much of our culture discourages us from looking at history and studying what social movements were about, so it's very difficult to develop the kind of commitment needed to build a movement today that is a solution to the problems on the scale that we are having to deal with, unless there is some knowledge or some way that we come to terms with what a movement is. And I'm just giving you some of my thoughts on it and I don't want to in any way suggest that this is the bible. You study it yourself, man; you guys go study it yourself. You glean it through all the experiences that you're going to come in contact with and help us collectively come to some kind of understanding of

Mural: "Without action there is no knowledge"
Highlander Research and Education Center
Photo: Katy Moore

what these times are and what they dictate in terms of movement.

When we look back on slavery and the anti-slavery movement, we don't realize that at the time of slavery, the struggle for a movement against slavery was very fragmented. Much was very vague in terms of what to commit to and what were the requirements of a social movement at that particular stage. If we kind of look back—all of us are abolitionists today, because that movement arose and it completed itself and found a solution to the problem of human beings owning other human beings. We can look back on it and say, that was what slavery was all about, and this is what happened in regard to the anti-slavery movement. Looking back on that movement you see its ramifications and its manifestations. You see that there was the issue of race; there was the issue of the role of women; there were the issues of foreign policy. Yes, slavery had a foreign policy. It also had a racial policy and a policy toward the role of women. It had a housing policy and a labor policy. It also had policies related to the issues of the environment; for instance, they would deliberately exploit and exhaust the land because of the rigorousness of cotton production. After exhausting the land, draining it of mineral resources, the cotton planters would then move further west and so on. They had an education policy that the slaves shouldn't read. Teaching the slaves to read was outlawed, and in some cases the punishment was death. They didn't want anybody to encourage the slaves to learn how to read. The slave revolt led by the literate Reverend Nat Turner had taught the slaveholders that the slaves must not be allowed to learn how to read the Bible. But there came a time in the struggle around these issues when it was made clear that all those issues and policies were tied to the fundamental problem of slavery, and the cause—that is, the ending of slavery and freedom—became the thing that amalgamated the different concerns and struggles into a powerful and successful Abolitionist movement.

Today, the tendency is to look at the various issues and struggles that are emerging and seeing them as separate. People enter into activity based on particular issues. And at first they do not have a complete understanding of what is defining these times as slavery defined the issues and ills of its time. They understand the leaves and sometimes the branches of the fundamental problem but not its roots. This precludes the consciousness and motion necessary to help galvanize and amalgamate a broad social movement. What is important to see, as was suggested yesterday, is that there's a connection between Ward's Island and Mountaintop Removal. That there's a connection between women and their children having to eke out some kind of living without a toilet—I can't forget that—and the connection between that and the war in Iraq. There is a connection! And leaders are the ones who identify those connections and understand the issues that tie these things together, that allows us to amalgamate the various fronts of struggles into a social movement. The Poverty Initiative is proposing that the issue that defines these times is the concentration of wealth on the one hand and poverty and the growth of poverty on the other. It's just putting that out there, not as the Bible—nothing like that—but for people to talk about and debate these issues and discuss them. And this is the thing that I think was very vigorous about this process: people begin to debate these issues, and discuss them. We have had some arguments—we have had some debates in the car, and that's okay. It's alright—especially now—for us to have differences. It's okay. Because that becomes the basis for us developing a deeper consciousness of what is it that defines these times and therefore what is it that we have to do in relationship to these times. Are these just isolated problems—that have no relationship to one another—that we have to deal with one at a time so we can all do our own thing and choose whatever we want to work on? Or are we dealing with a problem that is of a social character that requires a social movement? What we want to suggest from the Poverty Initiative, based on our studies and based on the experience we've had so far, is that we're dealing with a problem that's becoming worse, and it's of a social character, and it needs a social solution. We have a big problem, so we need a big solution, and that solution is a social movement.

Now looking at history, its clear that social movements inevitably develop in stages—very important. This is a very important understanding and conclusion to come to, especially in our culture, because we have this remote control type of mentality where we want to fast-forward to the end of the movement. We want to build the roof before we build the foundation. We don't see things in stages. When a woman says, "I'm pregnant," we want the woman to lie down on the table and start pushing right then and there. But the mother has to go through certain stages of the pregnancy. In order to be a midwife that facilitates that process, you have to figure out what is needed at each stage. For us to understand a social movement, we've got to understand these movements in terms of social stages. When we look at history we can see how those stages unfolded in various social movements and that the initial stage is one of crawling before you walk. And the crawling stage or initial stage is always one of identifying leaders and developing their capacity and their commitment. No matter how massive the activity that might be generated during that initial stage, the key question is who are the leaders that emerge and how do you bring them together and develop that kind of consciousness?

Also what we've learned is that a developing of a movement, in its initial stages, always starts with the telling of untold stories. The powers that be that have vested interest in the status quo make sure that there's a mega-narrative that everyone adheres to, but there are other narratives pushed into the background that are never heard—particularly the stories of those who are most victimized by that status quo. Movements get underway as those who are most victimized by the problem begin to tell their stories or to set the conditions where their stories are being told. Part of the incentive for these Truth Commissions is to get the unheard to say what they have to say, and to have the old notions and ideas and stereotypes, especially, to be challenged by the voice of the voiceless. This is very important, and I know with the Poverty Initiative one of the roles that we really see ourselves playing, given the nature of seminaries, is that we can help set an environment where leaders connect up, and where their voices can be heard; they can hear one another, and we can hear them, they can hear us, and we begin to generate the kind of leadership development process to complete this initial stage.

Lastly, I want to talk about some of the other things that we've come to understand in terms of history of social movements. One is the role of culture and then the other is the role of the church. I don't know, but my experience tells me—and when I look back and study history, history tells me—that you cannot have a social movement that involves increasing segments of the population—that has impact on the rest of society—without culture, without music, without singing, and without dancing. These become a way that you attract and impact other people and build a movement. I think all of us here—with just this little short experience—have seen the role that the music has played and the role that culture played. The performance that Derrick gave us—that was powerful stuff, man. This stuff moves you. You have to be made out of steel or wood not to be moved. Culture and music—it's just absolutely indispensable. It's not just entertainment. It's a way you get the unheard stories told, the untold feelings felt. This is absolutely crucial, and those of us who have the talents, artistic talents, it's incumbent upon those of us who have the talents—artistic talents—to fight this question through leadership in this particular area. All successful social movements take on culture and music as strategic matters—indispensable matters in its development. That's what history tells us, and I think we need to take that up in terms of our studies and also be very very perceptive in terms of when we see how that's manifested in our experiences and the experience of various movements. Okay, that's the role of culture.

Role of the church: I mean, the role the church and religion play is different in different cultures, but in my study of world history and in the experiences I've had just in the embryonic stage of our process, its clear that religion serves as a real shaper of the values, of what's important in people's lives in this country. And in the core values of our country, this aspect of religion and the role of the church is crucial. When you look at all the struggles, you can see how this thing has played a role. We hold these truths to be self-evident. Everyone's created equal. And they are endowed by their creator with certain inalienable rights. And among them is the right to life, liberty, and the pursuit of happiness. This is a paraphrase. Governments are constituted to ensure that these rights that are endowed by our creator are carried out, and if government abdicates that duty, it is our responsibility—it is our right—to rectify the situation. When we pledge allegiance to the flag—from elementary school through high school—these are the values we're pledging allegiance to. These are the values everyone in our society has been ingrained with. These are the things we need to appeal to. You can see the role of religion in that process, and in order to move people you have to respect that and appeal to that. And the role of the church is crucial in this process; the role of religion is crucial. It is not something that you can just dismiss because its not what you're into. The movement is about you, but it ain't about you. I remember being in a tent city with the Kensington Welfare Rights Union. We had 30-something families staying in these makeshift tents and shacks we put together, and we put this tent city on a busy street that everyone uses so they would come by and see us. We were trying to bring attention to the issue of homelessness, and kids being homeless, and all that kind of stuff. And we caught the imagination of many churches of all the different denominations, and I remember one day there were about 10 religious groups of different faiths that came to give us donations and stuff. Every time they gave us a big donation, before we got the donation, we had to pray. Man, I had my head down praying all that day. Man, I had a crink in my neck I prayed so much. I've never prayed so much in my life. I wasn't a Pentecostal—that's not my particular religion—but I respected that for the people that were. I wasn't Muslim—we had Muslims. I had to respect that. I had to understand that, and move with it. Religion, in our estimation, based on our experience, is so key. And if you think about some of your experiences, I believe you'll see the critical role of religion and the church. As these poor communities are devastated, the church is often the only institution that people have to go to in order to get some kind of redress. We've got to come to terms with the church and the role of the church, and those of us—especially those of us in the seminaries—have to think about this aspect of social movements.

These are aspects of a social movement—what has to be brought together and knit together by leadership—that I wanted to put on the table for consideration as we think about where we go from here in terms of each of our commitments and as we figure out what we're going to do about the problems that are happening on our watch. Like Larry said, "Don't waste my time, man." You know, we're talking about people's lives here. People hear me?

Joe Strife
Highlander Research and Education Center
New Market, TN
Photo: Alix Webb

View from the lawn of the Highlander Research and Education Center
New Market, TN
Photo: Katy Moore

Alix Webb (standing) speaks to the Immersion participants gathered in the meeting room for group reflection
Highlander Research and Education Center
New Market, TN
Photo: Adam Barnes

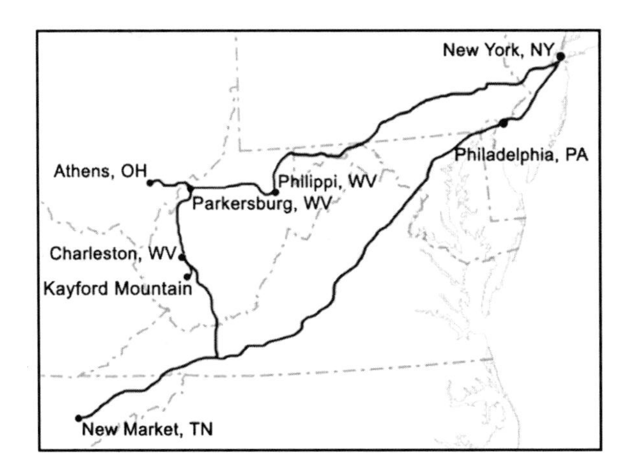

Sunday, January 14

Chapter 9

Itinerary:

Return the rental vans and board coach for drive to Philadelphia and New York with a stop for lunch in Salem, Virginia.

Sunrise at Highlander Research and Education Center
New Market, TN
Photo: Sarah Smith, Media Mobilizing Project

Justin Ward
Union Theological Seminary

Abby

I met my new friend Abby on a Sunday afternoon. After attending worship at her church in West Virginia, Abby's minister invited me to stay for pizza. There were many people in the fellowship hall that afternoon, but for some reason, Abby and I just gravitated to each other.

Abby is seven-years old and like me, she loves to talk. In the hour and a half that we gabbed over pizza, I could barely get a word in edgewise. Her smile never faded from her face during our time together. She delighted in telling me about many of the things that bring joy to her life; in fact, it's all she wanted to talk about. She spoke to me at length about her love for horses and designing outfits for her sisters to wear in fashion shows around the house. She told me she plays the guitar and even writes her own songs. Abby's life is busy and full. One day she hopes to become a famous fashion designer or an actress. Hers is a smile I would love to see grace the cover of a magazine.

A few minutes into our conversation, I couldn't help but notice that Abby had sandals on her feet, the kind I would never choose to wear when it's cold outside. "How could Abby be so happy, wearing sandals in January," I thought to myself. She didn't even have on socks, but still, she never complained about being cold.

I can't recall how it came up, but Abby later volunteered that she doesn't have any sneakers. The only shoes she owns are the sandals she had on and a pair of snow boots that her parents got her for Christmas.

Toward the end of our time together, I decided to ask Abby who she admired more than anyone else in the world. Her answer was no surprise.

"My mom," she said.

Later, when I shared Abby's response with her mother, tears started to roll down her cheeks. She embraced her little girl and then looked at me and said, "Thank you." "Thank you."

A few days passed, and our trip through Appalachia was almost over. But for me, the best part of our trip was yet to come. As we boarded the bus to head back to New York, our driver told us that we would be stopping for lunch in Salem, Virginia—a town that's about forty-five minutes away from the place I call home. I picked up my cell phone and called my mother immediately. Having met Abby and her mom, I was eager to wrap my arms around my own mom and thank her again for all she's done for me.

Like my new friend Abby, I also admire my mother more than anyone else in the world. Abby helped me to remember why.

My mother has always had an obsession with scarves. In fact, I can't recall too many times that I've seen her in public without her makeup and a scarf. At Christmas time, I always ask my mother what she'd like and inevitably I get the same answer: a scarf. She always looks beautiful, my mother, but until last year, I had never quite been able to figure out what the deal is with the scarves.

The scarves, she told me, make it so that she can wear the same outfits over and over again, without anyone noticing. Like Abby, I grew up poor without ever knowing it. My father left our home when I was in the second grade and my brother in Kindergarten. My mother, a schoolteacher, was suddenly left with a mortgage payment and two little boys to take care of all by herself.

How she did it, I do not know. Teachers in some states barely make enough money to support themselves, let alone a family of three. It was faith, I suppose. And not only did she manage to raise us, we never went without anything. But she did. As new school years would begin, my brother, Carson, and I could always count on a few new outfits and sneakers to keep up with our growing bodies. Except for a new scarf from time to time, my mother rarely ever bought anything for herself. I now know that if she had, my brother and I would have gone to school without lunch money. Mom always packed her lunch with leftovers from the night before.

During the sixth grade, my mother decided that our family would fly to New York for the Junior High National Chess Tournament. My brother and I felt like the coolest kids on the chess team when our flight attendant gave us our angel wings. Several years later, when I asked Mom how we were able to take that trip, she said, "We weren't" and proceeded to tell me it took her years to pay off the credit card she used to purchase the plane tickets.

Justin Ward (right) with his mom, Mattie Ward (center) and Bill Malashevich (left) during our break for lunch.
Salem, VA
Photo: Selene Kaye

Like Abby's mother, my mother did without so that I wouldn't have to. I know there were many times when she thought we would not make it, but she walked in faith and did the best she could.

I sense that God is calling us all to do the best we can, for what more can we really do?

Richard Greenlee, Ada Adamson, Larry Gibson, my mother and Abby's, have all been confronted with uphill battles. Their challenges have not disappeared overnight, but somehow they have summoned the strength to live in faith and do the best they can. Each one of them is persistent in hope and lives each day of their life as if it's their last.

Where in your life are you being challenged? How strong is your faith? I've seen that faith gives birth to possibility. Faith can stretch dollars and raise children; faith may ultimately signal the end of mountaintop removal. And it's because of faith that people are moved to end poverty.

What can your faith help you to do?

Though the full impact of our actions can't always be seen or measured, there does seem to be at least one guarantee. If we sit back and choose to do nothing, nothing will happen.

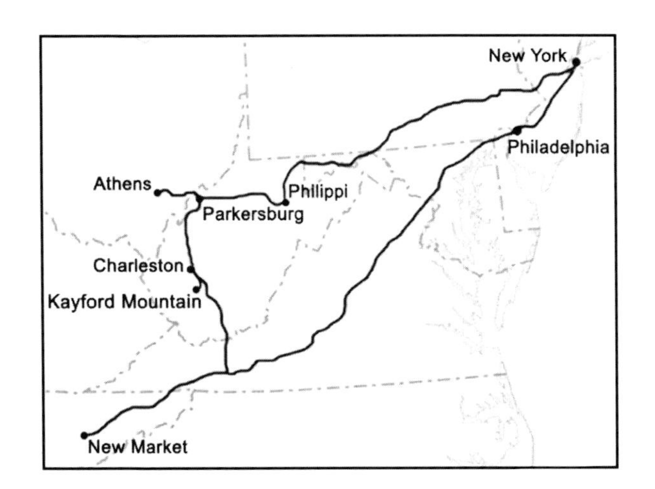

Looking Back, Going Forward

Chapter 11

Jan Rehmann and John Wessel-McCoy lead a sing-a-long at a post-trip community dinner.
Poverty Initiative Office
Union Theological Seminary
New York, NY
Photo: Colleen Wessel-McCoy

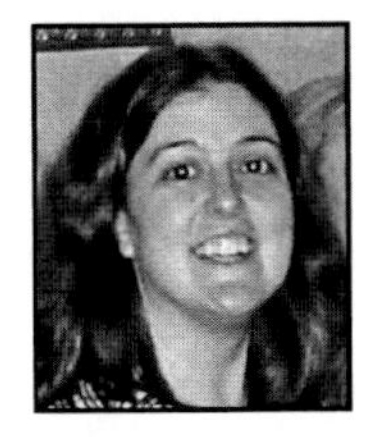

Liz Theoharis
Union Theological Seminary

A Growing Movement to End Poverty

I was sixteen years old the first time I saw mountains. They were the mountains of Greece where my grandfather grew up. He was a shepherd there and came to the United States (illegally) in search of the "American Dream." He knew how to make his own cheese and wine and he grew, raised or caught what he needed to survive. At first my grandfather did okay in Milwaukee, Wisconsin where he settled. And then the Great Depression hit. His "American Dream" became a nightmare—the nightmare of poverty that is so prevalent and growing today in the United States.

Wealth inequality is at an all time high in the United States and the world. Two thirds of the world's population lives in desperate poverty. Millions of people in the US are homeless. More than sixty million people go without health care every year in the US. In fact Martin Luther King, Jr. said during the Poor People's Campaign that he launched in December 1967, "Of all the forms of inequality, injustice in health care is the most shocking and inhumane." It was with these statistics and the human lives that make up these statistics in mind, I traveled to West Virginia, Ohio, and Tennessee on our Appalachia Immersion Course in January.

The first thing I saw in West Virginia were mountains, lots of beautiful mountains; I met people who live off the land and grow gardens and hunt animals to eat; I learned about poverty and hunger and illness and pollution; I witnessed profound suffering and even stronger resistance and organizing; I was reminded of my family.

And just like my grandfather who lived off the land and worked hard to provide for himself and his family, the families of Appalachia are working hard to provide for their families. But the coal mines and employers, and other conditions, are making it difficult for people to live.

While in Appalachia, I learned that the largest employer in the state of West Virginia is Wal-Mart. Wal-Mart has worked out a deal with the state that they don't have to pay taxes for fifty years. That means a smaller tax base to support the schools, municipal services and other social programs. Wal-Mart means more poverty in West Virginia. Wal-Mart has emerged as a primary employer there as the coal mining jobs have disappeared. Decades ago there used to be nearly 200,000 people who worked in the mines. Today, with long-walling, strip mining and mountain top removal, only 17,000 people mine even more coal than decades ago. Most people in West Virginia cannot afford the natural gas and other forms of energy that they produce. While the coal mines have clean water and electricity, many of the folks who work those mines and live in the same mountains have polluted water and no electricity. And poverty continues to grow. I learned that the population of the women's prison has quadrupled since welfare reform. Many of these women are in jail for economic crimes—forging checks, stealing, selling drugs, and other crimes related to poverty.

But what's happening in West Virginia is not isolated to West Virginia alone. Poverty is deepening everywhere. The week after I returned from our Appalachia Immersion trip I traveled to New Orleans. In the Gulf Coast, I learned that hundreds of thousands of people have not been able to return to the City of New Orleans since they evacuated for Hurricane Katrina. They have not rebuilt schools or health care centers, let alone housing. They are tearing down public housing at the same time as poor people have nowhere to live. Service organizations have built a dozen or more homes in the Lower Ninth Ward and other poor communities, but there are thousands and hundreds of thousands of people who need housing, jobs, and services. The people of the Gulf Coast as well as the people of Appalachia are being left behind. Their American Dreams have also turned into nightmares.

Two weeks after our Appalachia Immersion trip, I traveled to Detroit, Michigan where poverty is worsening as well. Every year since 2000, between 40,000-45,000 households in Detroit have had their water shut off. This means that hundreds of thousands of people in Detroit have no potable water. This is in a world that is made up of two-thirds water. While I was there, they announced that they are closing down fifty-two public schools in Detroit. In 2006, over 200,000 home mortgages were foreclosed in Detroit. The policies around eviction are getting tighter. People are living in more and more desperate situations. The brothers and sisters that I visited in Detroit see a connection between their struggle for water and housing rights and the people of Appalachia and the Gulf Coast; they are working to connect with groups from communities across the country struggling for change.

Since the Immersion course and my trips to New Orleans and Detroit, I have been in Baltimore, Maryland and Chicago, Illinois. I have spent time with organizers from New York City, Ithaca, New York and Washington, DC. In all these places, poverty is becoming the dominant contradiction in this wealthy land—people evicted, social services cut, job conditions worsening. These conditions are impacting more and more families. However, in the face of this misery, poor people are fighting back. In all the places I have visited in the past few months—West Virginia, Ohio, Tennessee, Louisiana, Michigan, Maryland and New York—I am witnessing the birth of a social movement, rooted in the culture of the places where I have traveled and based in the communities that are directly impacted by downsizing, destruction, displacement and other forms of degradation. This movement is needed if we are going to change the worsening conditions and make the United States the beautiful paradise and dream it could be for all residents. In order for this movement to grow, I hear the challenge of the people of West Virginia to take a stand for justice and I commit my life to the betterment of all.

Gathered for reflection
Highlander Research and Education Center
New Market, TN
Photo: Selene Kaye

Shawnee, OH
Photo: Colleen Wessel-McCoy

Sara Suman
Columbia University School of Social Work

Coal & Berries

When I first told people that I was going to the Appalachian region of the United States, I got some very interesting reactions. Some said, "Why the hell are you going there?" Some said, "Be careful of those hillbillies, they are very scary, they kill people you know." I challenged this reaction by saying, "How do you know, where are you getting that from?" They often responded with something similar to, "I saw some television show a while back." This is what I was hearing from "educated" "urban" folks, supposedly sophisticated and cosmopolitan in their worldview. Their responses reflect a provincial attitude that they're projecting on isolated groups in this society. They assume that we city dwellers are more evolved, more intelligent and that somehow the isolation and poverty of US rural areas are distinct cultural phenomena related to the peculiar quirks of, in this instance, the Appalachian people. Our painful lack of political and economic understanding that prevents us from recognizing the poverty of Appalachia is inextricably linked to the wealth of New York City.

One speaker on our journey shared with us this quotation: "West Virginia is the bastard child of political rape." He explained to us that West Virginia was created for the purpose of setting up an internal colony. The mineral rights were bought up by coal companies in the early twentieth century which defined "the right to mine and remove all of said coal, and with the free and uninterrupted right of way into, upon, over and under the said land, at such points, and in such manner, for such ways, tracks and roads as may be necessary and proper for the purpose of ventilating, draining, digging, mining, operating and carrying away said coal." In other words the people of Appalachia have to do the dangerous work of extracting the coal, but the coal companies, whose offices and owners are in Pittsburgh or New York, reap the financial benefits.

From the beginning the Appalachian people were frequently denied the opportunity to benefit from the natural resources of their own land. I see striking parallels all over this country and all over the world. It is the nature of a globalized free market economy to exploit indigenous workers and the land for labor and natural resources. In California, migrant farm workers are paid an unlivable wage under inhumane working conditions to work the land that at one time belonged to their ancestors. They are treated as uninvited guests who must accept inhumane treatment in order to stay working and survive. It is their toil, their energy, their labor that allows California to be the sixth largest economic superpower in the world with a Gross State Product of over $1.5 trillion according to the California Department of Finance. They who work the land do not benefit from this payoff, nor does the area or land that bore the berries, walnuts or lettuce get anything for its generosity. It is only tilled again, responding to the demands to produce ever more for an economy on steroids. The money that migrant farm workers should receive for their work goes to Los Angeles or San Francisco, to CEOs, high-level managers and shareholders. If the extra money going to coal companies and agra-business is not going to pay for worker's food, housing, medical bills and other basic living needs, then where is it going—a pool, a bigger house, fancier food, the best liquor money can buy, a private doctor who makes house calls, private yoga classes because the stress on the job is just getting to be too much?

We may not be the CEO or the high-level manager but we are implicit in ecological and human exploitation in other ways. We are living in a society that is allowing for the working under-class to become more and more invisible. Perhaps we believe that as long as we do not think about those who do the "dirty work" of coal extraction and strawberry picking the injustices they endure do not exist. We do not worry about them because we pretend that our fancy spring mix salad just appears on our plate with snap of a chef's fingers. We plug in our cell phones, computers, leave lights on when we are not in a room because we are not thinking about the natural resources required.

It is easy to get overwhelmed by all the injustices in the world and it is hard to know what to do about it. I strongly believe that it is our job to tell the truth. Our journey into Appalachia presents us, and all whom we came in contact with, an opportunity to engage or re-engage in a struggle against power and exploitation and build and strengthen the growing movement to end poverty.

Ben Sanders III
Union Theological Seminary

If Only Because

Can I do anything to eliminate the injustice that exists?
The answer to my question was clear:
I must do something!

If only because
this kind of poverty baffles me to the point of personal anger,
I must do something!

If only because
I know that there are millions of people living in poverty that are,
like my mother,
too proud to speak up about their situation,
mistakenly believing they are in poverty alone,
I must do something!

If only because
I know that there are still children in Chicago,
and all over the world,
who walk to school with frost-bitten hands as warm buses and cars pass them by,
I must do something!

If only because
I was once left out in the cold,
and I continue to live one school loan away from being back outside again,
I must fight,
with my whole life,
to do something.

Coal in Chestnut Ridge
Philippi, WV
Photo: Sarah Smith, Media Mobilizing Project

Stefanie Schoen
Union Theological Seminary

Preserving Our Strength: Environmental Education as a Means of Strengthening Resistance

Larry Gibson, the last inhabitant on Kayford Mountain, near Charleston, West Virginia, is determined not to sell his land to a coal mining corporation. He has been offered $150 million and his life has been threatened, yet he refuses to leave his "poor" home. Where does such steadfastness come from? Why does this man live a recluse-like life on his mountain top while the mountains around his property are systematically removed?

Why did Candy, after serving in the US Air Force, return from Turkey and Florida to her small town in Appalachia, embedded among the mountain ridges, instead of staying in the "sunshine state?" Candy, a young local organizer and single mother of three sons, would say: the value of family and tradition along with her commitment "to work for a better life for 'my kind'" were the reasons why she did not leave Appalachia for good. "My kind" was the phrase that this descendent of Native Indians used very often in order to emphasize social ties; yet I sensed that her roots might go even deeper than that. During our stay Candy never explicitly mentioned her connectedness to the beautiful landscape and nature of Appalachia as a reason for staying and as a source of inner strength. She would have said that her strength in life comes from her belief in Jesus Christ. She almost seemed to be offended when a student asked her if nature has a particular impact on her beliefs. She would vehemently refuse to see any connection between her inner strength and the fact of being rooted in nature: "I know that some native Indian tribes worshipped trees," she said, "but not my tribe! 'My kind' always believed in Jesus Christ the Savior." She was determined to prove that she or "her kind" was not pagan—whatever this would mean in this context. I, however, strongly wonder if Christianity and the belief in nature are really mutually exclusive.

Together with Candy and a minister from World Vision, a small group of students went on a three hour trip along the "ridges." The program for this day was supposed to focus on "Time Banking," a social concept where neighbors establish solidarity by putting their skills and talents to work in exchange for the work of other neighbors. The ministers from World Vision have chosen Candy to be the person to establish a network among the residents of Philippi, West Virginia, for whom she obviously cares. Every place we visited on our trip that afternoon, Candy knew all the names, all the stories, all the family relations as well as all the conflicts among neighbors. Having grown up in this close community that has existed for centuries, she knew all their (hi)stories. Candy herself is part of the ongoing history of this place in Appalachia, a beautiful hilly landscape which was settled by Cherokees—Candy's ancestors—before European settlers arrived. No doubt, relationships with people—not only "her kind"—are central in Candy's life. However, it turned out that these relationships and memories were not only entwined in family histories and a sense of community. Spending time with Candy it became more and more obvious that rather than free floating in a vacuum, all her childhood memories and stories about relationships were deeply embedded in the hills, rivers, rocks and trees around Philippi. "This is the rock where my mother and I used to take a sun bath on hot summer days!" and "Look, there, this is the place where we used to have barbecues with our friends." She pointed enthusiastically to a place on the riverbank which was flanked by a huge rock and trees lining the river. "And here, can you see the rocks in the river? My father wrote our names on them, when we were children...Look, here is my name: 'C-a-n-d-y'...and this is my brother's name," her outstretched finger pointed to enormous rocks resisting the river's wild water. It seemed as if she knew a story about every place there. "We used to body surf down this part of the river," she explained. "Man, that was so much fun... I wouldn't recommend it to you though because you don't know the stream and you don't know where rocks are lying close under the surface. I would jump into the water from this rock over there. But don't do it yourself; you might break your neck because you don't know the river." Joy and pride sparkled in her eyes. This was her territory. She knew it. It was her treasure. She was convinced that you have to have grown up in this place to understand it the way she does.

Candy Adams and Stefanie Schoen
Chestnut Ridge
Philippi, WV
Photo: Alix Webb

"'My kind' has never settled in the city center of Philippi", she explained. Racially considered "black" by white residents, "her kind" have lived on the mountain ridges, girdled by rivers and trees. Today, being among "city people" this knowledge was hers. Only hers. Knowledge is power.

Some days later we visited a place near Charleston, West Virginia. "Follow me", said Larry, a small man in his fifties, wearing jeans, a baseball jacket and cap. "I'll show you a place where I used to play with my cousins. You won't believe your eyes." Like Candy, Larry's memories were directly connected to the landscape where he grew up. To our utter dismay, however, the playground of Larry's childhood—unlike Candy's—had fallen victim to a far-away, profit-oriented, large coal company named Massey Energy Company which is systematically removing the mountains in order to obtain coal.

When I saw this hideous "destruction site" I felt like I was in a bad science fiction movie. Knowing personally what it means to experience childhood adventures and develop friendships outdoors in a beautiful natural setting, my breath and words were taken away. It was unbelievable: enormous ear-piercing rattling excavators and giant freight trucks literarily removing a mountain. Larry's words hit me like a hammer, "If they can take away my land, they can take away yours as well, if they smell profit there. We really are living in a material world." If we don't stand in solidarity with people whose rights are violated, we give up our own rights and, even worse, we give up our belief in human rights.

I've been studying as an exchange student in the US for half a year and so far have not felt homesick nor the need to go home even for Christmas. Yet, while on Mount Kayford, vivid pictures of my own home, a small village in a rural, "economically weak" region in Bavaria, Germany embedded in low mountain ranges (the Fichtelgebirge in the North and the Bavarian Forest in the South) came to my mind and tears came to my eyes. The further I go away from home, particularly when I move to university cities, the more I realize that nature, the rocky and rough surface of the hills, the steady trees and the unhurried flowing rivers are not only the substrate of all the deep "philosophical" discussions with my best friend but also have left their profound imprint on my personality and even my language, a deep Bavarian dialect which always reminds me of the roughness and warm down-to-earthness of the landscape and the people that this landscape has brought forth.

I found a similar love of his Appalachian dialect in Dr. Greenlee's speech. He grew up under poor conditions and is today a professor of sociology at the Ohio University in Athens. Dr. Greenlee still holds on to his dialect, even though his language is frequently considered "uneducated." This language represents home for him. One could feel him shivering inside when he gave his talk in which he said that this region, people, culture and language are often called poor and backward. This inner emotion was far more than being nervous about giving a talk in front of a large group of "city people" he had just met for the first time. It was a holy anger about a mentality that deprives his "poor" culture of its dignity by spreading a false image of a retarded, violent, lazy and ignorant people permanently stuck in the past. It showed the extent to which he cares about his origin—the people as well as the landscape.

In one sense so vulnerable, like Larry and Candy, he stood in front of us like a rock. Like Larry and Candy he knew why he was standing there and he knew what he cares about: Appalachia and the kind of straightforward, genuine and down-to-earth people who this rough region has created and nurtured over generations.

I vividly remember a moment during my time in Bavaria, recalling my own memories of a childhood in a beautiful rural countryside while singing the verse of the hymn "We shall not be, we shall not be moved, just like a tree planted by the water, we shall not be moved." This image of an unmovable tree illustrates for me how education by and in nature makes people strong and resistant. It illustrates how people recognize their dignity and are empowered to steadily stand up for their rights by envisioning the beauty and strength of a high grown tree that has its fixed place where it is nourished and to which it belongs. Above that, I understood that this verse describes solidarity: I understand not only that a tree would of course never leave the place where it is planted but also that the similarity of the experiences of Candy, Larry, and Dr. Greenlee to my own experience of life in a rural place with beautiful mountains, rivers and trees made me feel a deep connectedness and solidarity with these people who were brought up on another continent from mine.

Despite all the similarities of our childhood experiences, however, I have realized throughout my stay in the US that the idea of a sustainable, environmentally friendly lifestyle seems to be in contradiction to the "American Way of Life." Unfortunately, the average daily energy consumption of one single person in the US is five times the world's average and twice the daily consumption of a person in Japan or Germany. Some of this energy comes from the coal which is mined behind Larry's house. Yet on our trip it was also obvious that Larry and Candy are not alone in deeply appreciating and caring for the nature around them; there are people organized in the umbrella organization "Rural Action" in Appalachian Ohio, including several VISTA Volunteers, who are working on alternative farming, creek restoration and other environmental projects.

But how can we think about environmental education and protection when people worry on a day to day basis about how to make a living? I questioned our priorities when I heard about a Environmental Education Center located in a poor neighborhood in the suburbs of Prague, Czech Republic. As a volunteer there, however, I learned that environmental education is not a luxury that only rich people can afford, but that it empowers parents as well as kids through experimental and experiential learning about amazing ecological coherences and sustainable lifestyles. People started to grow their own vegetables and thought about healthy but inexpensive nutrition; they developed exciting outdoor rallies and learned how to do handicrafts from natural material in order to spend time together. They began to reduce waste, brought their own bags for shopping and became more conscious of valuing and saving water and energy. They figured out that this knowledge does not only help to protect nature but helps them to develop responsibility and a strong personality. More than that, it often also saves money. If you educate the children, they will never forget what they have internalized and they will pass it on and apply it wherever they go

What can be learned from an environmentally conscious lifestyle as well as from nature itself? We can learn to care for the earth in all its complex dynamics. What I learned during our Appalachia trip is that it is so much more productive to watch out for the already existing beauty and richness of the earth [and its people] instead of looking for deficiencies, always keeping in mind that it is under no circumstances a luxury to preserve what preserves us.

Chestnut Ridge
Philippi, WV
Photo: Alix Webb

Philippi, WV
Photo: Selene Kaye

Adam Barnes
Union Theological Seminary

Why Don't You Just Move?

I spent two years living in Niger, West Africa. Niger consistently ranks near the top of the United Nations' list of least developed countries.[1] Nearly ninety percent of Niger's population is rural and relies on agriculture. The country is four-fifths desert, 4% of the total land is arable, Niger is land-locked, there are periodic droughts and plagues of locusts, and it has one of the highest average temperatures on the planet.[2] When I would tell friends and family these facts about Niger I would watch as they listened and mulled over the problem in their mind. Most were quick with a solution and one of the more common solutions was posed in the question: Why don't they just move?

Appalachia is one of the poorest regions in America and is continuing to get poorer.[3] The development of new mining techniques and the expansion of mining operations in the western United States have contributed to a loss of coal production and coal mining jobs in Appalachia over the past several decades.[4] The geography in much of the region consists of dense hills, narrow valleys and only a thin (average three inches) layer of topsoil, making agricultural prospects dim. As I've been asked before, why don't they just move? I put this question to a native of Appalachia, Professor Richard Greenlee of Ohio University in Athens. He responds:

> I'm not sure that the written word can convey the true meaning of this place for those who have not experienced it. It is HOME, and if you love home, and home provides you with meaning and purpose in life, then why would you want to leave it? HOME is everything (family, friends, nature, faith, music, art, sports, community, etc) that has taken place over generations. It is your roots and without roots there is rootlessness. It truly is an existential experience and when one leaves it there is a vacuum of emptiness that follows. When you are here you are filled with a sense of meaning that is all consuming. It is not about POVERTY, it is about a richness brought about by the immersion of self into a culture that no

[1] United Nations list of Least Developed Countries (LDC), 2003
[2] C.I.A. factbook, 2007
[3] Appalachian Regional Commission (ARC), Keystone Report, 2005
[4] Coal Production in the United States, Energy Information Administration (EIA), 2006

amount of money can replace. It is a very powerful concept that seems to have been lost on much of the world and its people.

Whether it is Niger, West Africa or Athens, Ohio, one must carefully consider the implications of leaving a place one calls home. Above all, there is, as Greenlee points out, an existential connection that people make to a place. Over the generations land becomes part of the lived memory; it is the place of struggle, sorrow, joy, birth and death. The memories and the rhythms of the place become sacred to those who live there. By leaving this, sanctity dies and one must readjust to a foreign, unfamiliar, oftentimes hostile, environment. Moreover, moving to a more prosperous area does not necessarily translate to increased prosperity for the individual or family that moves there.

These things should be fairly obvious to anyone who can imagine themselves in a similar situation. But, because someone can, in all sincerity, suggest to someone else, "You should just move" indicates there is a much broader ill. It demonstrates that there is an unequal relation of power between those who can give this advice and those who are asked to consider it. It says that people who are poor have made bad choices and that since people like me who are unpoor have not, we (unpoor people) can tell them (poor people) how to fix their situation. It presumes that poor people never considered the possibility of moving, never anguished over the fact that they weren't able to find work and provide for their family, that they are too stupid or stubborn or sentimentally attached to their home to move.

I believe this attitude is often not adopted malevolently but is a result of individual and systemic weaknesses. By offering the poor an explanation for their poverty, one is able to make the poor person's plight a fixable situation. Therefore, if they have not done all they can, the poor are to blame. This attitude is then reproduced, reinforced and made acceptable by the various tactics and strategies of a society that makes choices for the poor and not with them. These weaknesses allow me and many others to avoid the proper, individual human response which might lead to doing something to change it.

Multicultural Genealogical Center
Chesterhill, OH
Photo: Erica Almiron, Media Mobilizing Project

Charon Hribar
Union Theological Seminary

Wisdom and Strength in Appalachia

Before going on our trip to Appalachia, our class was continually reminded of the need to be active listeners—to listen to the stories of the people and to learn from their experiences. We were also called to reflect upon the stereotypes we have held about Appalachia and to confront our misconceptions as we traveled through West Virginia, South East Ohio, and Tennessee. It was listening to their experiences and sharing our own stories with the people whom we met that enabled us to build relationships with the people living in Appalachia. One question for our hosts that arose on our journey, a question that seemed vital to ask before returning to New York became, "What is it that you want others to know about Appalachia?" The response that most vividly lingers in my mind from many people whom we met along the way is,

"We are a community that survives."

The strength, the endurance, and the spirit that was expressed by the people of Appalachia continue to inspire me. The people whom we met were frank—they knew the perceptions that people outside of Appalachia had of their people, and through our encounters they confronted these stereotypes. Taking the time to sit down and talk with many different people in Appalachia enabled me to see the truth of their experiences and forced me to move beyond the lies perpetuated by a one-sided history that we have been taught in our schools and through the media.

Richard Greenlee, a native of South Eastern Ohio and now a professor at Ohio University gave a dynamic talk about the stereotypes that have plagued the people of Appalachia. He said,

"We have an image problem in Appalachia—how others see us."

Prof. Greenlee's talk was painfully honest. While his initial rejection of Appalachian stereotypes seemed to be a blunt attempt to debunk such stereotypes, as he continued to dig deeper into his own experiences of growing up poor in Appalachia, he began to unveil the pain that permeates an individual when she/he has internalized such stereotypes. Prof. Greenlee expressed the embarrassment he has experienced because of who he is. His stories caused me to reflect on my own experiences of poverty. While I did not grow up poor, I do come from a working class family that knows the hardships of poverty and from parents who never wanted their children to experience the adversity they had to endure. I come from a family that knows how to survive and wanted more than anything to live out the "American dream." But what does that mean—to know how to survive, to pursue the American Dream? What stereotypes does such a dream create about those who do not fit the mold of a white, Western, patriarchal society? What pieces of ourselves are we required to repress or destroy in order to "succeed" in such a society? Prof. Greenlee's story of leaving Appalachia and then returning to become a professor made me reflect on notions of success that are propagated in this country.

Prof. Greenlee explained that while he has never felt at home in the academy and that he still can't believe he is supposed to be there, what he has experienced since leaving Appalachia has isolated him from his roots. The culture that once nurtured and sustained him, has in some way become foreign to him, or rather he has become an outsider to his native culture. Prof. Greenlee's reflection caused me to remember times in my own life when I wanted to reject pieces of my past and made me think about the shame I have at times felt about myself and my own family. Today, thinking about the way I was conditioned by society to value "success" and the way such conditioning made me embarrassed about my past both enrages me and brings me to tears.

So what is the role of academia in reinforcing such ideologies of success? What is it about education that has forced Prof. Greenlee to live in limbo? I am not trying to devalue the importance of education, but rather I am confronting the scope and breadth of our educational systems. When we begin to realize that the "History" (I could also include the Theology, the Philosophy, the Literature...) being taught in our school systems is the history of only a small minority of the people who make up our country and our world, I believe we must begin to question the values and "expertise" that are being reinforced through our educational systems. We must critically reflect on whose knowledge we being asked to ascertain. When we recognize the way in which white, Western, patriarchal paradigms are perpetuated under the guise of liberal, democratic education, we must turn to the knowledge of those who stand beyond the boundaries of a white, Western, patriarchal reality and bring their stories to the forefront of education. I believe this is what Prof. Greenlee is working to do through a program he has created at the University of Ohio called the Appalachian Scholars program. While our society continues to strip people of their culture in an attempt to reinforce a "melting pot" vision of the United States, Prof. Greenlee has refused to give up his bond with the people and land of Appalachia. He recognizes the knowledge and strength that exist in his culture and is lifting up this knowledge within the academy. I believe this is what the Poverty Initiative is working to do; to break down the barriers of academia and lift up the knowledge held and analysis being done by poor people whose voices are continuously marginalized in our society.

While our society seems to demand that we take on an identity that is not our own if we are to succeed in the United States, the Poverty Initiative is working with groups of organized poor people across the country who refuse to give up the richness of who they are and who refuse to be plagued by the stereotypes which have been imposed upon them. The Poverty Initiative has taught me that one of the first steps to eliminating poverty is recognizing the human dignity of all persons through the telling of untold stories and the building of relationships. It is for this reason that Prof. Greenlee's comment on the demoralization of the poor in our society spoke such volumes. He suggested that the poor in our society are forced to pay the price of being poor with their dignity and their souls. If we sincerely value every human person and if we are truly in relationship with one another, then we will begin to understand how the price paid by the poor is the price paid by all. When one is forced to suffer through injustice in order to survive, we are all suffering from injustice. When we realize that our lives are intimately connected, we will no longer be able to justify the oppression people are forced to struggle against It is for this reason that we must learn to stand with the poor of Appalachia, of the Gulf Coast, of New York City, and of the world and embrace people for all that we are. We must create genuine solidarity in our society by learning from one another and by acknowledging the wisdom that exists in our diversity.

Tygart River
Philippi, WV
Photo: Katy Moore

PETER CAVA
Union Theological Seminary

"You Have the Answer"

9 January 10007 A.D.A.[1] (Waning Gibbous Moon): Chestnut Ridge, West Virginia

> Rocks do indeed make a sound. All things that the Great Spirit has put here continually cry to be heard. The problem is, there are few who listen.
>
> — Agnes Whistling Elk in Lynn V. Andrews, *Spirit Woman*

Candy is not from Philippi. Candy is from Chestnut Ridge—the other side of the mountain. In other words, she is a Melungeon, looked down upon by many for her mixed European, African, and American Indian descent.[2]

Candy takes members of the Poverty Initiative to see Chestnut Ridge.[3] On our way, we pass a large house, bought by a non-native and built up with many extensions. As we drive through winding hills, Candy tells us about the discovery of natural gas in the land. Candy laments that outsiders tapped the gas and that her people see very little of the wealth this generates.

When we arrive at Chestnut Hill, we see many clusters of small houses and hundreds of acres of land. The people here live by subsistence farming, Candy explains. The community is relatively poor but self-sustaining. When families become too large, they erect additional small houses rather than expanding a house.

---

[1] "A.D.A." = "After the Development of Agriculture." 1 A.D.A. = 8000 B.C. By dating my entries in this way, I seek to communicate that I see no sharp distinction between time before the birth of Jesus of Nazareth and time after the birth of Jesus of Nazareth. However, for clarity's sake, I use standard dating unless explicitly indicated. See Merlin Stone, "9978: Repairing the Time Warp and Other Related Realities," Heresies, no. 5 (September 1978): 124-6.

[2] Sources debate the racial composition of Melungeons. In this essay, I use the most widespread theory. See Rachel Rubin, "'What Ain't Called Melungeons Is Called Hillbillies': Southern Appalachia's In-Between People," Forum of Modern Language Studies xl, No. 3 (2004), 259-60.

[3] Although I narrate the events of this day in the first-person plural, I did not travel with Candy to Chestnut Ridge. Most of my information about Chestnut Ridge comes from Derrick McQueen, who did travel with Candy to Chestnut Ridge. Derrick shared his experiences with me in personal conversations on 9 January 2007 and 20 January 2007.

With a glow of excitement, Candy takes us down to see the creek. She shows us the rock where her friend's father painted her name twenty-four years ago. She shows us the rock where she used to bask in the sun with her mother, stick in hand to chase away the copper snakes. She shows us the rock that her family would use as an oven to cook meals during long, joyful days at the creek.

Finally, she takes us to a bridge where we can see the creek flowing down between two mountains. She tells us about how she and her childhood friends used to body-surf down the creek. She thinks that maybe her people should start a small-scale river-rafting business to attract tourism, bringing greater prosperity to the region. She fears, however, that outsiders may somehow buy up more of the land, take control of the business. She wants her people to remain in control of their destiny. She fears commercialization, build-up. She fears most of all that her people may one day be driven off the land altogether.

I touch a rock from the creek with my hands, and I listen.[4] The rock says:

> I give gladly to those, whether girl or serpent, who know me as home. But when I am dressed up in strange development and forced to give to those with whom I share no relationship—that is prostitution.

10 January 10007 A.D.A. (Waning Gibbous Moon): United Campus Ministry Center, Ohio University, Athens, Ohio; and the Monday Creek Restoration Project, Trimble, Ohio

> My vagina swimming river water, clean spilling water over sun-baked stones, over stone clit, clit stones over and over. . . .
>
> Not since they took turns for seven days smelling like faeces and smoked meat, they left their dirty sperm inside me. I became a river of poison and puss and all the crops died, and the fish.
>
> My vagina a live wet water village.
> They invaded it. Butchered it.
> And burned it down.
>
> I do not touch now.
>
> — Eve Ensler, "My Vagina Was My Village"

In the morning we travel to the United Campus Ministry of Ohio University. There, as we revive with a lunch of vegetarian vegetable soup, sociologist Bruce Kuhre makes a presentation in which he describes Appalachia as an

[4] Derrick McQueen brought back a small rock from Chestnut Ridge and invited me to reflect on the rock's experiences on 9 January 2007.

"internal colony," noting that approximately 80 percent of the land is controlled by interests outside the region. When outsiders control the land, Kuhre suggests, both the land and her inhabitants suffer. As an example, Kuhre displays video footage of black, slimy water coming out of a bathtub faucet, followed by an interview clip in which a local woman testifies, with some embarrassment, that water pollution from coal mining gives her and other women vaginal infections.

That afternoon, several of us visit the Monday Creek Restoration Project. Before underground mining, Monday Creek and the surrounding region teemed with mayflies, beetles, brook trout, spotted bass, and other wildlife. But acid mine drainage killed everything.

I listen for the earth to share her perspective:[5]

> The women of Appalachia endure vaginal infections, because I endure vaginal infections. I have been raped through underground mining, and I have been infected through the consequent flow of deadly acid.

The Monday Creek Restoration Project seeks to purify the water. Mike, a volunteer for the Project, tells us that due to the Project's purification efforts, local residents are spotting fish in the water for the first time in over a century. Members of the Project hope that the water will one day be swimmable.[6] However, acid will continue leaking into the creek for centuries still.

12 January 10007 A.D.A. (Last Quarter Moon): Kayford Mountain, Cabin Creek, West Virginia

> I have dreamed on this mountain
> Since first I was my mother's daughter
> And you can't just take my dreams away
> Not with me watching.
>
> You may drive a big machine
> But I was born a great big woman
> And you can't just take my dreams away
> Without me fighting.
>
> — Holly Near, "Mountain Song"

[5] Ted Bernard and Jora Young, The Ecology of Hope: Communities Collaborate for Sustainability (Gabrola Island: New Society Publishers, 1997), 169-71.
[6] Ibid., 169.

"What do you hold so dear in your circle of life that you wouldn't give it up for a price?" That is what Larry Gibson asks us when we visit him on Kayford Mountain. For Larry, the answer is the mountain herself. Although Larry has been told that by 2008, his mountain will be worth well over half a billion dollars, he refuses to sell.

Since this refusal, Larry has survived multiple murder attempts. Bullets knock the dishes out of his cupboards. His home has been terrorized, his truck vandalized, his dog shot. He lives with an existential awareness that his days are numbered: "I talk to everyone as if you are the last one—because you may be."

Larry shares great intimacy with the mountain. "The land talks to you," Larry tells us. "You've got to understand that a mountain is a live vessel." He reminisces about his childhood experiences of playing in a nearby waterfall. That waterfall is no longer here.

The waterfall, like so much of the surrounding landscape, has been destroyed by mountaintop-removal (MTR) mining ("peak reduction," as coal companies call it). As Larry describes it, whereas other forms of mining take the coal from the mountain, MTR takes the mountain from the coal. Larry refers to the line dividing his land from the land undergoing MTR as "Hell's Gate," because nothing beyond that line can live—not even the Chinese grasses imported by Arch Coal and Massey Energy to "restore" the land. Larry says that he could give us a pocketknife on his land, and we could live; but beyond Hell's Gate, he could give us everything, and we still wouldn't be able to survive.

Larry mentions that at one point an employee of one of the coal companies claimed to be Larry's kin. But Larry knew it wasn't true. Kin wouldn't support MTR. Larry eventually proved that the employee had lied about being kin.

Larry takes us to Hell's Gate. It is worse than any of us could have imagined. The land is disfigured irreparably. Knowing that coal companies use three million pounds of explosives against West Virginia mountains every working day;[7] knowing that over half a million acres of mountaintops have already been destroyed; knowing that for three inches of topsoil to form in the Cabin Creek area, the earth must work for three millennia; I stand at Hell's Gate.

I ask the land for her perspective:

> To remove a mountain is to sever my breast. How can I nourish life when I am dismembered in this way?

[7] See the pamphlet "Mountain Top Removal Destroys Our Homeplace." Larry distributed this pamphlet to members of our group.

We return to our cars, but we still hear the machines from beyond Hell's Gate. We gather into a circle and sing, "Let justice rain down!" On my cheeks, rain intermingles with tears as the earth and I weep together. The sound of the machines outlasts our song.

"If you don't do something about what you see, you shouldn't have wasted my time," Larry implores us. "You have the answer of what happens."

13 January 10007 A.D.A. (Waning Crescent Moon): The Highlander Research and Education Center, New Market, Tennessee

> I don't know exactly what a prayer is.
> I do know how to pay attention, how to fall down
> into the grass, how to kneel down in the grass. . . .
> Tell me, what else should I have done? . . .
> Tell me, what is it you plan to do
> with your one wild and precious life?
>
> — Mary Oliver, "The Summer Day"

We end our travels at Highlander, an activist center founded in 1932 by Don West and Union Theological Seminary graduate Miles Horton.[8] On Saturday, we discuss strategies for using our experiences in Appalachia to fuel and inform social and ecological activism when we return to Philadelphia and New York.

During an outdoor discussion about the role of cultural transformation in social movements, I stand up and walk out onto the grass. Not too long ago, such inspiring activists as Rosa Parks, Martin Luther King Jr. and Eleanor Roosevelt engaged in similar discussions at Highlander.[9] Did they comprehend then the tremendous impact that they would have on the world?

I look down over Highlander's landscape. Voluptuous mountains. Clitoral hills. Trees spreading their branches unabashedly. Erotic, not pornographic. Wind-whispers and birdsongs laughing away my memory of the drone of mountain-mauling machines. Organic, not mechanistic. Radiantly real.

Heaven's Gate.

The land calls out to me:

---

[8] See "History—1930-1953: Beginnings & the Labor Years," Highlander Research and Education Center, accessed 13 December 2006 <http://www.highlandercenter.org/a-history.asp>.

[9] See Myles Horton with Judith Kohl and Herbert Kohl, The Long Haul: An Autobiography (New York: Teachers College, 1998).

> Just as I give birth to this vegetation, I am giving birth at Highlander to an alternative future, a future rooted in a deep past, before my prostitution, rape and dismemberment. Will you labor with me?

19 January 10007 A.D.A. (New Moon): Union Theological Seminary, New York, New York

> "The good news may be that Nature is phasing out the white man, but the bad news is that's who She thinks we all are."
> — Alice Walker, "Nuclear Madness: What You Can Do"

After writing most of this essay, I take some time for final reflections. Being back in an urban setting after spending the previous week in rural areas, I recall that "at the rural stage of [the development of mythologies of the mother-goddess], we always find the mythology of a chthonic goddess, an earthly mother like Gaia or Rhea, while at the urban stage of development, we find an astral mythology, with the triple moon-goddess as its dominant figure."[10]

During my time in Appalachia, I did not consider the night sky's waning moon.[11] In many ancient mythologies, the waning moon signifies nature's destructive aspect, as well as the sovereign scale of fate or the thread of destiny. I sense nature speaking a final message to me about all that I saw in Appalachia:

> If humans continue to tax my body, I will need to abort the human species for the sake of my health and the good of my other children.

Life on earth will go on with us, or it will go on without us. You have the answer of what happens.

---

[10] Heide Göttner-Abendroth, "Thou Gaia Art I: Matriarchal Mythology in Former Times and Today," Trivia: A Journal of Ideas, no. 7 (Summer 1985): 66.

[11] The word "consider" derives from the Latin considerare, "to observe the stars" (Webster's Third New International Dictionary of the English Language, ed. Philip Babcock Gove and the Merriam-Webster Editorial Staff [Springfield: G. & C. Merriam Company, 1967], 483).

Lovelle Clark
Union Theological Seminary

So Many Battlefronts

On the last full day of our sojourn during the January Immersion trip to Appalachia, I typed a few paragraphs for the trip "blog" site; this was to be my entry, my contribution to the stories and recollections about the whole experience. I told several people that those three paragraphs were "primo" stuff; I suppose since I'm a poet and writer in general, I brought all of my skills to bear in that entry. Well! The darned thing got erased when the laptop on which I was typing gave a "powering down" warning. Turns out it was supposed to have been plugged into the wall, but somehow that got overlooked.

I mourned the loss of those sentences just as I would mourn the loss of a freshly-created poem that got similarly lost. (Which is why I write out all my new poems longhand before ever typing them at the computer!) But in the approximately three weeks since then, I have come to realize that, although that was some of my best, most lyrical, even poetic prose writing, it was not the right tone for what I wanted to say. I had entitled that short piece Living in Poetry. I spoke eloquently and whimsically about the beauty of the countryside around the Highlander Education and Research Center near Knoxville, Tennessee and of the center itself, which is where our group of forty-seven travelers were on that final leg of our journey, and, indeed, it was lovely.

However, the Highlander Center was a well-established, longtime-existing institution; they had had over eighty years to craft the buildings and furnish them in such a way as to elicit rapturous responses such as mine. Not wanting to take anything away from that most august, socially-conscious and –active, sorely-needed place, I must nevertheless share what Holy Spirit has placed in my spirit, mind and heart in the interim: I must speak about the "uglinesses" which I encountered and experienced during the trip as much as about the beautiful things, perhaps even more so.

Ugly things such as the bald-headed mountaintops all around the mountain which remains the property of a feisty little man (who is all of about five feet tall) named Larry Gibson, a mountain and a man which are the lone holdouts in this Charleston, West Virginia area; the US government and huge corporations have bought up all the land/mountains around Gibson's and blasted the hell out of them in order to get to the coal that lay beneath and within. Gibson spoke to our assembled party under the roof of a nondescript gazebo on a gray, dreary, rainy day near the end of our travels as his large, quite friendly dog waggled in and out among many of us as if we were long-lost friends. Because of my arthritis, I did not actually go with the others to what Gibson called "The Gates of Hell" to view the decimated mountains; still, I was able to envision how they looked from the reports of a few of my companions, and, even, without their reports, I could well imagine that the blown-apart mountains were not merely bald-headed, but had basically had their brains blown out! At this point in my life, I am painfully familiar with the extremely heavy handed, blunt-force trauma way that big business and uncaring government goes about getting what they want; I've witnessed it so often and in fact have experienced it in my own life.

Larry Gibson has a big white-painted wooden sign nailed to a tree on his mountaintop. It reads "Stanley Family Heirs" (presumably his family name) in big, black letters. Now, even though Gibson's mountaintop—with its ramshackle cabins and other buildings (including outhouses), its midwinter-sparse vegetation and greenery, it's forlorn, weary atmosphere (especially on this gray, rainy day)—didn't seem like anything so great to me, a big-city girl born and bred, still my heart leapt up within me as he spoke of never giving up and I felt a fierce, sudden protectiveness towards and pride in him at the same time that I felt hot, disdainful anger and contempt for those no-good folks who were trying to knock him off of his mountain. (They had killed his dog and performed other such dirty, demoralizing tricks in the past.) Although I've never owned a home nor any land, somehow I knew what it felt like to be threatened with having to leave your home and land, where you had lived all your life, when you didn't want to. Even though I couldn't quite see it—or at least I couldn't see myself cherishing that mountaintop as much as Larry Gibson did—still I recognized that, even with the surrounding wounded, bleeding and crying, dying landscape, on his own mountaintop Gibson was living in poetry.

However, the bigger picture was of this solitary man and of this lone outpost from the ravaging armies of governmental and corporate greed as a battlefront in the war against the ever-present, constantly-morphing yet never really changing Oppressor, with a capital "O." I felt somehow as if some of the younger members of our group—among them some of my Union classmates, students from the Columbia School of Social Work, and members of the Media Mobilizing Project out of Philadelphia—had not yet had so many encounters with the big "O" in their lives, and so this experience with Larry Gibson was quite shocking, disturbing and perhaps even emotionally overwhelming for them. Well, it was disturbing to me as well; it's just that I expected no less from the big "O," in whatever guise it appeared this time. This was just another instance of the multi-countenanced, seemingly all-powerful Oppressor exercising that power over the seemingly powerless oppressed. But that feistiness which Gibson displayed so forcefully and naturally, that righteous indignation, that belief in his cause as a just, honorable one—all of these things are loci of power.

Lest you think that the idealist in me has just run amok, let me say that—even with all of that belief in Gibson and in some others whom I met and interacted with during the immersion experience—nonetheless I frequently despair of their ultimate victory. As someone who is entering into a higher plane and into advanced initiations on my Christian walk/path, I believe more than ever in the ultimate triumph of good over evil in this spiritual warfare; however, I often experience, witness and fear the loss of what seem to be so many crucial battles in the meantime. But then Holy Spirit reminds me that I am here not to sail through life, at ease, unchallenged, and unencumbered; rather, I am here to fight the good fight of faith, at every juncture and in every way. Still, the world-weary part of me cries out, "But there are so many battlefronts!"

Battlefronts like the one at which the women and friends of DAWG (Direct Action Welfare Group) are fighting, women such as Evelyn, the founder of the organization—a pleasant yet definitely tough, sharp, organized person who (as a welfare mother) identified a need, planned how to address it, and took off from there. Evelyn has an admirable matter-of-fact way of looking at and dealing with issues, and I'm sure she and DAWG have enjoyed some good successes in their fight to obtain some basic human dignity, rights and resources. Of course, the big "O" is still out there (here?), so the struggle continues.

Another individual who was quite memorable for me is Beth, an administrator/social worker at the West Virginia Department of Health and Human Resources. A married woman with children of her own, Beth fights tirelessly in her job of working with families, trying to get for them the resources and services they need for a minimum standard quality of life. I was just so impressed with Beth's caring and compassion; she obviously isn't in it for the money, because she let us know that her salary isn't that great and, from some of the stories she told us, her job sounds as if it's frequently overwhelming, frustrating, and maddening (due to a limited, always-being-cut budget, bureaucratic red tape, etc.) But—she does it. I suspect a big part of it is that she thinks of her client families as members of her own family. And I more than suspect that she finds strength, wisdom, etc. to carry on from her faith because, at the end, right before we were going to leave, I asked her, and she confirmed that, yes, her faith was a big factor in her being able to keep going, to stay on the battlefront.

After experiencing this Appalachian Immersion trip with my fellow students and others, I came away initially somewhat shaken and despondent, wanting to be of more substantive service to my fellow human beings, my fellow oppressed folks, yet realizing that there are so many battlefronts and that some days I don't even feel like reporting for combat duty. Yet, Holy Spirit, in Holy Spirit's inimitable way, brought me along slowly over the past few weeks to understanding that "The battle is not [mine]; it's the Lord's"; that "'vengeance is mine,' says the Lord. 'I will repay'" [Those Oppressors who keep gleefully oppressing]; that "the battle goes not to the swift, but to [s]he who endures"; that, to paraphrase Larry Gibson, as long as there's life and breath in me, I will continue to fight, to struggle, to stand with my sisters and brothers who are oppressed and filled with righteous indignation ("How dare they treat a child of God so!") and to sing "I'm on the battlefield for my Lor-or-ord, I'm on the battlefield for my Lor-or-ord! And I promised Him that I would serve Him 'til I die, I'm on the battlefield for my Lord!" Hallelujah!!

Philippi, WV
Photo: Ellie Martin Cliffe

Odis Braxton
Photo: Sarah Smith, Media Mobilizing Project

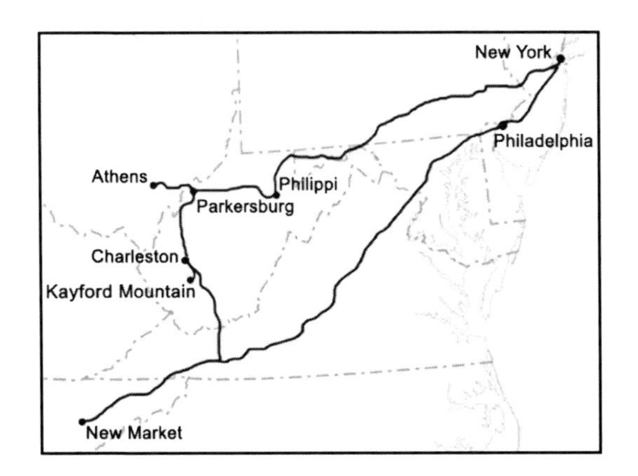

Race, Class and Poverty

Chapter 12

Robert Daugherty
Multicultural Genealogical Center
Chesterhill, OH
Photo: Quan Blanche, Media Mobilizing Project

Willie Baptist
Poverty Initiative

Poor Whites, Poor Blacks, Poor America

The Appalachia Immersion Course exposed all of us to a few of the unsung saints of the hills and "hollers" of the impoverished communities of West Virginia and southeastern Ohio. Their deep commitment and Davidic resistance against Goliathan odds inspired in me a greater devotion and a greater sense of dignity in the building of a mighty movement led by the 'least of these' to end all poverty and unnecessary human misery. This reaffirms the brave and broad mission of Union Theological Seminary's Poverty Initiative, the sponsor of this important Immersion Course.

The songs of the poor of Appalachia are the songs of all of Poor America, songs that Middle America is beginning to sing, songs that Katrina and FEMA made the world stop and listen. These songs are of an unjust and bitter fruit—abandonment in the midst of abundance. They evoked at once two conflicting feelings. One was of an "Oh, my God!" horror as in the response to the tortured image of a dead body hanging from a tree captured by the songstress Billie Holiday in her classic—*Strange Fruit*. And the other feeling was one of being challenged by Harlan County's Florence Reece who wrote of the courageous and righteous stance of the exploited coal miners in her unforgettable anthem, *Which Side Are You On?*

Whether it's the life threatening actions of the Automobile and Water industries in Michigan, the Coal companies' removal of mountain homes and polluting the environment in West Virginia, or the machinations of the Insurance and Casino businesses in Mississippi, a veritable warfare is being waged against the poor and displaced.

Despite the debilitating stereotypes portrayed by mass media and multi-billion dollar charities, poverty in fact has many faces. They are not only the faces of "underclass" blacks, undocumented Latino immigrants, and so called Welfare Queens. It is also the battered grimace of a "downsized" white father.

Many of the poor in West Virginia have been moved from Welfare to Walmart. Poverty has not ended. It has simply changed address. The much P.R.ed myth about the rich coal companies "bringing jobs to Appalachia" was challenged by a longtime fighter against mountain top removal. He recounted the fact that the coal industry has reduced their workforce over the years in Appalachia from nearly 200,000 jobs to less than 17,000 while continuing to amass mountains of untold private wealth. He exclaimed that, "If this is 'jobs creation', the coal companies must stop!"

Shaken by the many stories we heard on this Immersion Course, the story of a leading organization of poor families in West Virginia building a fight to end poverty especially moved me. This statewide organization calls itself, Direct Action Welfare Group—that is, DAWG as in "Dog." Evelyn Dortch, a founder and leader of the group, told of their relentless efforts to get aid to victims of Katrina. It was a description of a seemingly never-ending saga to overcome every barrier to reach their ravaged sister organization, the Louisiana Welfare Rights Organization. In the meantime, DAWG, despite its own "barely-making-ends-meet" existence, managed to raise $5,000 to send to their sisters in struggle. Now, here you have an organization of mostly poor white mothers of Appalachia worrying and leaving no stone unturned to come to the assistance of an organization of mostly poor black mothers of Katrina. Songs of such 'love-thy-neighbor' heroics are hardly, if ever, heard! But they should and will be!

While visiting the men's homeless shelter on Ward's Island on Friday, January 4, several immersion participants noticed these words of advise posted prominently on a shelter bulletin board:

In many cases it is easier for
a person to find causes or reasons to fight to
change the system
instead of finding the courage to
face and fight to change
the damaging lifestyle and
negative attitudes
that may have been part of the cause for
them being in the system.

Don't waste time trying to
change the system.
Do what you need to do to get out
of the system and into an
independent "positive lifestyle."

Brought to the attention of the group by John Wessel-McCoy and submitted by Alix Webb

Ben Sanders III
Union Theological Seminary

Poverty and Race: A Reflection on Appalachia and America

On Sunday during our trip we worshipped at the People's Chapel in Chestnut Ridge, near Philippi, West Virginia—a non-denominational church. After worship we headed over to the church's community center. While there we had lunch and then worked with the Media Mobilizing Project (a group from Philadelphia that traveled with us) to capture some of the testimonies of the congregants on camera. As we sat getting to know each other, I had a conversation with a woman who was a member of People's Chapel. Her husband was a Black man and she told me this way: "My husband, he's like you, he's your race." I understood that she was trying to get me to understand that she was married to a Black man; however, her choice of words leads me to an important question.

Her statement that her husband was "like me" is important inasmuch as it reflects a dominant way of thinking that reifies human identities (and human value) based on the color of one's skin. So, there I was in Appalachia learning about poverty and its history in this region while also being reminded of the centrality of race in America. As I sat and reflected on this conversation I reconfirmed a thought that I had had many times before: dealing with the construction of race and racial politics in the United States will be vital to any concerted effort to end poverty.

The question that jumps to the forefront is: what does it mean to work to end poverty that affects people of all colors in a country where race has historically been used to divide all people and to dehumanize and kill people of color? This is a complicated question and this article will not be long enough to sufficiently answer it. Instead what follows is a truncated answer to this question based on facts that I learned in Appalachia and statistics from the US Census Bureau, and my own hope that a courageous, prophetic love might have the ability to undercut racism.

Appalachia: History and Poverty

The point of our trip to Appalachia was to learn more about the reality and functionality of poverty in the United States in general and in the context of Appalachia in particular. Having grown up poor, the reality of poverty was not something I was unfamiliar with. However, the historical events that have created Appalachian poverty were astounding to discover. What this history says about the value of poor people in America, regardless of skin color, is powerfully important to working to end poverty.

Appalachia is extremely white, and much of the Appalachian region is extremely poor. That white poverty exists was something that I knew before the trip, but when we arrived in Appalachia I realized how little white poverty I had seen. Historically, the region is rich in many ways. From its musical tradition, which reflects the lasting cultural impact of European immigrants and African slaves, to the historic covered bridge in Philippi, the site of the first land battle of the Civil War, Appalachia has a rich narrative to tell.

Appalachia also has a history of being an area rich with natural resources, especially coal and timber. However, the relationship that citizens of this area have had to these resources is a major cause of the impoverishment of the area. The timber has been almost completely stripped away and while coal mining still provides work for some citizens, the act of mining is now being done to the detriment of the environment and Appalachia's mountainous landscape. Even worse is the fact that the people profiting from the timber and coal of Appalachia are not the natives of the area, but big business. Big businesses that do not suffer from the polluted water that follows coal mining, and do not care about workers that are forced to work for low pay and without the benefit of a Union. The economic condition of Appalachia is a clear reflection of how poor people of all colors are valued (or not valued) by the US government. A look at the state of poverty in the United States only confirms the devaluation of the lives of poor people in this country.

A Note on "Standards" of Poverty

One issue that must be pointed out before continuing is the inadequacy of the way poverty is defined. The standards used to measure poverty in the US are decades old and have not kept up with the changed percentage of the cost of food, housing, etc. Instead of explaining all of the technicalities of these inadequacies, I want to point out the ridiculousness of trusting rich people, people who have often never dealt with poverty personally, with the responsibility for determining what poverty is and how to mitigate and ultimately eliminate it. As long as the people who decide what constitutes living in poverty are the same people that profit from unaccountable wealth and power, poverty will remain a murderous reality. Instead, any movement that intends to eliminate poverty must be led by the poor, as the Poverty Initiative asserts.

Race and Poverty

The reality for many poor people of color in the United States is that racism and poverty are never separated from each other. The connection between racism and poverty is historically rooted. After all, the United States, and its legacy of white supremacy, is still profiting from the genocide of Native Americans, a systematic execution of the original peoples of America, and chattel slavery, a murderous and dehumanizing institution that still affects

Blacks today. Both of these institutions were predicated on philosophies that dehumanized non-whites in the economic interest of rich Europeans. The eras that followed, filled with white terrorism, Jim Crow and institutionalized racism all contribute to the continued impoverishment of people of color.

According to a US Census from 2004, 12.7 percent (approximately 37 million) of the US population is living in poverty. Meanwhile an astounding 24.7 percent of Blacks in America are living in poverty. This is compared to 9.8 percent in the Asian community, 21.9 percent in the Latino/a community, and 8.6 percent in the white community. That the United States government would allow nearly a quarter of its Black and Latino population (approximately 9.4 million) to live and die in subhuman conditions is disgusting. Yet, in the name of justice, it is equally disgusting that approximately 21 million white people are also living and dying in poverty.

One of the myths that allows the rich in this country to get richer is the idea that racism and poverty are completely separate issues. Dr. Martin Luther King, Jr. understood the importance of demythologizing the relationship between race and poverty. In his historic speech at The Riverside Church in which he challenged the United States' role in the Vietnam War, King spoke on "the giant triplets of racism, materialism and militarism" that we must defeat. King understood that poverty and racism (and militaristic force used by powerful nations) worked together to dehumanize poor people of all colors. Understanding the interconnectedness of poverty and racism informs my reflection on how lessons from Appalachia can be used to fight white supremacy.

Using Lessons from Appalachia to Fight White Supremacy

My experience in Appalachia reified the existence of the myth of racial superiority and inferiority that America is largely built upon. The tension that floated between me and the woman from People's Chapel as we spoke about her Black husband testified to the unfinished work of race relations in this country. There are still many conversations to be had, and we as a country still have much to learn about the courage that is required to love across racial lines. This need to love is not just a romantic hope; I did not leave Appalachia wishing for a multiracial circle singing "Kumbaya." Surely the destruction and reconstruction of race in America will require much discomfort, strain and tears.

Yet, if Dr. King was right, and I believe that he was, any effort to debunk racism must also seek to debunk the economic interests that have deep roots in the America's racial politics. The American Dream, as Malcolm X once pointed out, is the American Nightmare for many. Malcolm X was referring to the nightmare that Black Americans experience. I would submit that poor people of all colors also experience America's nightmare.

As I continued my conversation with this woman, we went on to talk about the reality of poverty in Appalachia. We spoke, as did many others, about the fact that living in poverty and being unemployed is dangerous to the life of anyone, no matter what color the person may be; that poverty will kill anyone with inadequate health care, regardless of skin color; that an empty stomach grumbles no matter the color of the skin; that babies without food or medicine die, regardless of skin pigmentation; and that the United States government is content with allowing these lives to pass away so that fewer people can stake claim to more resources. It is in this common place of constantly facing death due to our government's refusal to affirm the lives of all of its citizens where we must begin our work of creating a better future.

My choosing the elimination of poverty as a starting point for destroying white supremacy is not intended to belittle the importance of racism. As a Black person I understand that the state of Blacks in America is despicable, from the HIV/AIDS epidemic, overcrowded prisons, inadequate schooling, police brutality and much more. There is plenty of evidence that shows that racism in America is alive and well. However, talking with folks in Appalachia has confirmed my belief that poor people, because of the existential urgency caused by poverty, have the capacity to work together, not only to eliminate poverty, but also, in fighting side by side in love, to bring about a new conception of race that honors the right to life above the value of a dollar and above the color of one's skin.

(left to right) Union Theological Seminary
student Lovelle Clark with Sharron Witherspoon,
Patricia Wray, and Evelyn Dortch of DAWG
Charleston, WV
Photo: DAWG

Ella's Song[1]

We who believe in freedom cannot rest
We who believe in freedom cannot rest until it comes

Until the killing of Black men, Black mothers' sons
Is as important as the killing of white men, white mothers' sons

That which touches me most is that I had a chance to work with people
Passing on to others that which was passed on to me

We who believe in freedom cannot rest
We who believe in freedom cannot rest until it comes

To me young people come first, they have the courage where we fail
And if I can but shed some light as they carry us through the gale

The older I get the better I know that the secret of my going on
Is when the reins are in the hands of the young, who dare to run against the storm

We who believe in freedom cannot rest
We who believe in freedom cannot rest until it comes

Not needing to clutch for power, not needing the light just to shine on me
I need to be one in the number as we stand against tyranny

Struggling myself don't mean a whole lot, I've come to realize
That teaching others to stand up and fight is the only way my struggle survives

We who believe in freedom cannot rest
We who believe in freedom cannot rest until it comes

I'm a woman who speaks in a voice and I must be heard
At times I can be quite difficult, I'll bow to no man's word

We who believe in freedom cannot rest
We who believe in freedom cannot rest until it comes

---

[1] Derrick McQueen taught the group this song, which became a common refrain when we would sing together each day. Words by Ella Baker, music by Bernice Reagan. Submitted by John Wessel-McCoy.

Eva Gordon with kids from People's Chapel
Chestnut Ridge Community Center
Philippi, WV
Photo: Selene Kaye

Jessica Pulido
Columbia University School of Social Work

Appalachian Experience

The Appalachian immersion experience has opened my eyes in many ways. I have lived most of my life with a certain notion of what poverty is in the United States. Now, after my experience in Appalachia, I realize I was wrong and that there is still so much for me to learn and understand. There are so many things going through my head right now and I am having a difficult time articulating them so I will try to write what I am experiencing right now as best as I can, realizing that I am not through processing; and I may never be done processing my experience. The following is my experience as I understand it a month after coming back from Appalachia.

I am a Mexican-American female who grew up in Los Angeles in a working poor family; my parents worked but for the most part we lived from pay check to pay check with little money to spare. I had a good childhood, but I also realized that we weren't able to afford the luxuries that other children my age took for granted. I did not understand that I was poor until high school when I was unable to purchase the outfits that were in style at that time. As I began to understand that I was indeed poor, I also realized that most of the people that were in my same situation happened to be minorities while most of the "white people" in my classes came from money. These revelations shaped my view of poverty in the United States, and ever since then I have linked poverty with being a minority or a person of color. Although before the trip I had heard about "white poverty" I did not think of it as a great problem. Now I realize that I had been so focused on my people and their needs that I excluded so many others, failing to validate their struggles along with ours.

The Appalachia immersion program interested me because I wanted to find out more about "white poverty" and, in the back of my mind, to compare it with my experiences. I left New York doubting I would be able to relate to the people of Appalachia; I was so very wrong. For me, the defining moment of the immersion program was Prof. Greenlee speaking of his personal experiences in poverty. His story blew me away.

After a long day of meeting people and seeing different organizations, I was sitting in a nice little room having dinner with the rest of the group. I knew a professor was going to speak to us regarding Appalachia, but I did not know what the content was. After dinner, when a well dressed white man went to the front of the room and started speaking, I thought to myself, "Man, I have to sit through another lecture given by a professor. I already get enough of this at school. I hope he doesn't take too long so that we can leave."

Prof. Greenlee is an academic, but he grew up poor in Appalachia. As he related his story I was amazed that so many of his experiences were parallel to my own. Like him, I know how it feels when your parents had to ask for help in order to take care of the family. I remember the shame one sees in their eyes. I know what it is to have a parent come up with creative ways to make things work and have the family pitch in to help. I know what it feels like to want to buy a favorite teacher a gift but not being able to and instead giving her some trinket from home. Like Prof. Greenlee I know the feeling of getting into college and changing the way you speak in order to survive higher education and be accepted by your peers and professors. I know of feeling like you are always trying to catch up in class and fearing embarrassing yourself in front of others. Most of all I know what it feels to be stuck in the middle: no longer fitting in with your family, but never really fitting into your new world, wanting to have both worlds but really only having parts of them.

Shock does not even begin to describe my feelings when I realized that I was sitting in this room relating to and understanding the experiences of a white man. After Prof. Greenlee's talk I understood that poverty does go beyond race, and that I need to accept the fact that there is "white poverty." I am sad to say that I was guilty of not validating "white poverty." I have always sought for people to validate the fact that many minorities were poor and that things needed to change, yet here I was excluding this group and doing to them what others have done to me. I understand that poverty can be colorblind, even in the United States, and that I need to take into account everyone's suffering and not being so focused on claiming poverty as "just" a minority issue when it truly isn't.

I learned so much on this trip and met so many wonderful people, Now I realize that there are tremendous challenges out there that I—and many other people—will have to overcome in order to make this a more just society, including getting others to understand that poverty is not "just" a minority issue but one that affects many people of all colors.

Colleen Wessel-McCoy
Union Theological Seminary

Identity, Commitment and Transformation

> It ain't where you're from; it's where you're at.
> –Rakim and Eric B "In the Ghetto"

In its mission statement the Poverty Initiative asserts it is "committed to developing leaders who will build a movement, led by the poor, to end poverty." The significance of this emphasis on the leadership of the poor struck me when I first heard Poverty-Scholar-in-Residence Willie Baptist point out that just as it would have been absurd for men to lead the women's revolution or for white people to lead the civil rights movement, it would be wrong for non-poor people to lead a movement to end poverty.

This belief in the leadership of the poor is not a naive assertion that by virtue of being poor a person is qualified to be a leader or that one's intimacy with poverty makes one's analysis of the causes of poverty accurate, just as being a woman does not automatically give one a trenchant critique of patriarchy. Similarly, not being poor does not preclude a person from being thoroughly committed to ending poverty, just as being white does not prevent you from having a well-studied understanding of racism. Commitment should not be confused with identity. Commitment often follows identity (i.e. people of color are more likely than white people to have spent time analyzing systemic forms of white supremacy and be involved in dismantling them), but identity does not determine commitment (i.e. not all poor people have developed a critical analysis of the causes of systemic poverty and joined together with other poor people in organized resistance to those causes.)

It is not impossible for the rich man in Mark 10.17-22 to follow Jesus, to make that commitment, but he doesn't. He need only cast his lot with Jesus and the disciples, joining them on their way to Jerusalem, the seat of power, in challenging the current order. But it will mean giving up all of his riches, and as it turns out those riches are where the rich man's commitments lay. (This is where Jesus adds, "It is easier for a camel to go through the eye of a needle than for someone who is rich to enter the kingdom of God" (Mark 10.25)). It's hard to ignore how the story of the rich man contrasts with the example that follows in Mark 10.46-52: poor Bartimaeus sitting on the margins, though blind, sees clearly that his future is tied up with the Jesus movement. "Throwing aside his cloak," (v.50) thereby leaving behind a possession that would have been as valuable to a poor man as riches would have been to a rich man, Bartimaeus "jumped up," came to Jesus, and joined the group in their mission. The rich man's identity did not preclude him from making a commitment to Jesus, but it made it less likely. Bartimaeus' poverty and marginality from society did not automatically make him part of the Jesus movement, but it did help Bartimaeus realize that he had nothing to gain from sitting quietly beside the road and everything to gain from joining with Jesus in changing the world.

In *God of the Oppressed*, James Cone writes we "cannot see the radical and political thrust of Jesus' person and work" when our "vision is committed to the very structures that Jesus despised" (p. 205). Whenever I perceive that my interests lie in the maintenance of the structures that organized poor people are dismantling, I will be unable to recognize God at work in the world today. God is the liberating force in the midst of the resistance of the oppressed. To know God, we must know this struggle. To know this struggle, we must participate in it. Jesus is where people are resisting oppression, and that is where we must be. Wherever our identity tends to be a barrier to our commitment to justice, we must be strangers in our own land. We must endeavor to be like Ruth, the Moabite who is willing to go with Naomi into Judah, a land that is not her own, where she becomes the foreigner. Like Ruth clings to Naomi, must we cling to those who stride toward freedom, professing to the oppressed, "Where you go, I will go; the risks you encounter, I will encounter; your people will be my people; your God (of the oppressed) will be my God." This transformation, for which and out of which we must constantly struggle, is a conversion from allegiance to current systems of power to allegiance to the oppressed and the God of the oppressed.

The tendency for commitment to follow identity is related to privilege, particularly privileges that correspond with identity. If I benefit from a systemic bias, I am less likely to be able to see that inequality, and even if I do recognize it, I am less likely to want to change that inequality. Because being white does not bear negatively on our life chances, white people frequently miss the continuing significance and extent of racism. Because white people benefit from racism and white normativity, we have a disincentive for dismantling those systemic inequalities. Our white identity makes it less likely that we will be committed to ending white supremacy.

At the same time learning about the histories and realities of movement building and social change has complicated my understanding of privilege. Where does attention to ones own privilege help us make commitments that might seem counter to our identity and where does it inhibit good work? When does an emphasis on privilege prevent people from seeing their own economic vulnerability?

I am not rich, but I do have securities people who are poor sometimes do not: a warm dorm room and a key to lock the door, health insurance, education, the ability to live far from my family and still visit them for holidays, clean drinking water, and good food. But how secure are these things? When we attempt to name the privileges of sex, race and class, we often end up describing situations where rights are satisfied for some but not for others. Access to health care, housing, nutritious food and fair employment are rights. When we construe the difference between having health care and not having health care as a difference of privilege, we loose our grounding for making the satisfaction of everyone's right to health care a social priority. At their root the inequalities of access to health care are not based on scarcity, but on our failure to make access to health care a social priority.

The tendency to describe rights as privileges is closely tied to the myths that make the pervasive poverty and oppression ignorable or tolerable, that encourage us to presume that our current economic and social arrangements are natural and inevitable. Though my passions are Christian ethics and theology, there have been moments when I believed I could better serve economic justice by earning an advanced degree in economics. But this thinking succumbs to the illusion that only those with advanced degrees in economics are qualified to make decisions about our economic wellbeing. Our challenge to hegemonic neoliberal ideologies not only stems from a sophisticated parsing of neoclassical economic theory, but also from questioning the fundamental assumption that markets can and should be unencumbered by ethics or social values. Significant changes in our economic structure will require transformations in the way we interpret the world around us, so in the pursuit of justice, new ethical frameworks are an equally important corollary to new economic models. We must have both.

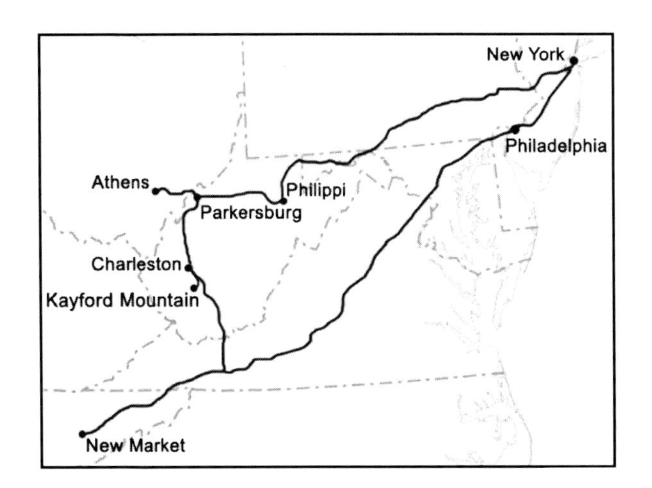

Coming to Terms

Chapter 10

Downtown Philippi, WV
Photo: Katy Moore

Jessica Chadwick
Union Theological Seminary & Columbia University School of Social Work

Going Home

One of the hardest questions for me to answer is when people ask me where I'm from. Not because I'm ashamed or embarrassed, but because I'm not sure. We moved a lot when I was a child. By the time I was twenty-two I had lived in six different states. I don't feel native of any area. I have many homes.

On the first day of the immersion course we were asked to introduce ourselves including, of course, where we are from. I said that I call West Virginia one of my many homes. I attended four years of college at Alderson-Broaddus and fell in love with the area. Lots of people in NYC often think that I am "from" West Virginia. I guess because I talk about it so much. Sometimes it feels disingenuous to talk about West Virginia as my home. What makes a place your home anyway?

In preparing for the trip I was nervous about taking people with me back to visit places in West Virginia that I knew and loved so well. We stayed the first four nights at my alma mater and visited with community folks, agencies, and professors that I have deep connections to. I was nervous and felt responsibility for how both groups would receive each other. It's hard to invite forty-seven people so deeply into your life. It feels really vulnerable.

At many points on our journey, I was scared of how this group of seminarians, social work students, and media organizers would interact with the people and community that I love so much. And some days it was hard. Some days, when people offered feelings and critiques of work that was being done, I got defensive. Its like when you can complain about your family 'till the cows come home, but God help anyone else that tries to say something bad about your family.

On the other hand, I understood that this is a process and a learning experience for our group to better understand the region, the connection to religion, and various models for eliminating poverty. I knew that many times I had the same critiques that members of our group offered. I know how important it is to process and question things that we were experiencing.

This question of "home" kept coming up throughout the trip. Many of the people we spoke with, shared with us how people outside the community have used the Appalachian region's resources or have come to proselytize or to exploit the communities. People are skeptical of outsiders, and rightfully so. As one not native to WV, what right do I have to call this place "home?"

During our textual reflections on the book of Ruth, the question of insider/outsider and the question of where is your home was also raised. Ruth follows Naomi back to a place where she is a foreigner and dependent upon others for her livelihood. Ruth vows to her mother-in-law that she will follow her and accept her people and her way of life.

On Thursday, in Charleston, Rev. Watts asked our group how many people felt called to ministry in West Virginia. I raised my hand. Since moving to New York city I have felt called to return to Appalachia. Then on Friday we witnessed the "Gates of Hell" as Larry shared with us the horror stories of mountaintop removal. That seemed to seal the deal for me. It is clear to me that I must, at some point, return to West Virginia to continue to work to eliminate poverty. It is my calling: to this work and to this region. After seeing the destruction of the earth and of people's lives in the name of capitalism, how can I not go back?

Like Ruth, I vow to enter a land that I am not native to, but that I consider my "home." "Your people shall be my people..."

Sara Suman, Peter Cava, Liz Theoharis and Jessica Chadwick play basketball with youths from People's Church
Chestnut Ridge Community Center
Philippi, WV
Photo: Erica Almiron, Media Mobilizing Project

Ben Sanders III
Union Theological Seminary

How Much

Wednesday night, after finishing a long day, we met at a Presbyterian church in Athens, Ohio for dinner. Many of us were exhausted. We had not slept much the night before, we had been in cars all morning and much of the day, and we had spent the day traveling around different locations in southern Ohio. We were hungry, sleepy and irritable. I had spent my afternoon with a group of others from the trip, reflecting on the passage of my ancestors through the Underground Railroad. Standing in a Quaker cemetery, I had also reflected on the delicacy of life and the tragic pain of death. I just wanted to eat my lasagna and sleep. Yet as I began to turn my brain off for the evening, we were challenged even further by a dynamic presentation from Dr. Rich Greenlee of Ohio University. He asked, will we continue to perpetuate the ignorant, stereotypical viewpoints of poor people in rural areas? His presentation was a brilliant display of personal testimony and academic research.

But I was tired.

After Dr. Greenlee's presentation we loaded up our caravan of vehicles and headed to Parkersburg, West Virginia where we would sleep for the night. As I drove I thought about how tired I was and how much work there was to be done. Poverty is an enormously complex issue, I was exhausted, and I thought to myself, "Can I really do anything to change the injustice that exists?"

The answer came to me through my exhaustion. Dr. Greenlee had made me think of things that I did not want to think of. One memory in particular stands out. I remembered being in first or second grade and having my fingers frost-bitten during a long, cold walk to school. Public bus after public bus passed by my mother and me, but we just walked. This was the middle of a Chicago winter, the temperature was about fifteen degrees, in the season before the freezing cold wind blows and sends the temperature easily below zero. We were both wearing very thin gloves that did little more than cover our hands. I told my mom my hands were cold, then I told her they hurt; she told me to keep walking. By the time I got to school my hands were so cold they felt like they were burning (strange I know, but I'll never forget this feeling). At the school my mom and I went into a bathroom and I put my hands under some warm water and this only made my hands hurt more. As I cried from the pain, my mom told me to keep quiet, she didn't want anyone to hear me and find out about our long walk. Dr. Greenlee was right when he talked about often not wanting to ask for help in the midst of poverty.

The answer to my question (Can I do anything to eliminate the injustice that exists?) was clear: I must do something! If only because this kind of poverty baffles me to the point of personal anger, I must do something! If only because I know that there are millions of people living in poverty that are, like my mother, too proud to speak up about their situation, mistakenly believing they are in poverty alone, I must do something! If only because I know that there are still children in Chicago, and all over the world, who walk to school with frost-bitten hands as warm buses and cars pass them by, I must do something! If only because I was once left out in the cold and I continue to live one school loan away from being back outside again, I must fight, with my whole life, to do something.

John Wessel-McCoy

Mountain Music, Freedom Songs, Murder Ballads

> Then the coal company came with world's largest shovel
> And they tortured the trees and stripped all the land
> Well they dug for the coal till the land was forsaken
> Then they wrote it all down as the progress of man.
>
> From "Paradise" by John Prine

Is it horrible that "We Shall Overcome" gets on my nerves? Time and again I've tried to learn "Solidarity Forever" and found a powerful resistance within me—a feeling of cynicism for these old songs of struggle. I am a union organizer and I don't like singing union songs. I may own the Little Red Song Book, but I must confess that there's hardly a song within its pages that I've been able to commit to memory. I can sing neither "The Internationale" nor "There is a Power in a Union" by heart.

Not too long ago, I noticed that most of the songs I could sing by heart were dark and violent. The most troubling part was that I seemed to have a partiality for murder ballads—"Banks of the Ohio," "Pretty Polly," "Omie Wise," and "Long Black Veil" to name a few. The murder ballad tradition has deep roots in American music—from blues to bluegrass. A murder ballad delivers just what you might think: a tale of deadly violence sometimes concerning lovers and sometimes rivals. Whatever the relationship between killer and victim, it tends to be a very intimate story.

Consider this verse from the "Banks of the Ohio":

> I took her by her lily white hand
> Led her down where the waters stand
> There I pushed her in to drown
> And watched her as she floated down.

This is not what I'd call positive and uplifting. Why did "Banks of the Ohio" appeal to me enough to learn it while, for the life of me, I can't get passed memorizing the first verse of "Which Side Are You On"? My own personal issues with folk music aside, these murder ballads have survived centuries, passed on from one generation of musicians to another. I'm not the only one who finds something compelling in their lyrics. For example, folks in Appalachia have been singing some version of the ballad "Pretty Polly" for centuries. Before it arrived in the Appalachian Mountains, folks in the British Isles were singing it.

On the question of what songs to sing, Woody Guthrie said: "I hate a song that makes you think that you are not any good. I hate a song that makes you think that you are just born to lose. Bound to lose. No good to nobody. No good for nothing." I wish I could be more like Woody, but here I am singing these morbid tales of tragedy and violence. There's something in them that feels true to me. In the last verse of "Pretty Polly," Willie, the murderer, ends the song with, "Gentlemen and Ladies, I bid you farewell / For killing Pretty Polly my soul will go to hell." There's no bigger way of losing than being bound for hell, but then again, Willie has just murdered Polly. His violent act demands condemnation.

This matter of violence brings me to our journey through Appalachia. We walked through what Larry Gibson of the Friends of the Mountains referred to as the Gates of Hell—the fence marking where his land ended and the coal company's property began—and we reached the rim of a mountain that no longer exists. In the abyss below, we could see machines biting into the rock and hauling away the mountain by the truckload. In this sight, I saw something horrible yet familiar.

When I worked as a case manager for a supportive housing program in Chicago, there were times when I would find the corpses of clients with whom I had worked. It was not uncommon for a client to die alone in his or her room. Living in isolation, living a hard life, living with addiction, living in poverty—these were the circumstances held in common for all those whose lonely deaths I discovered. No one I ever found was the victim of a murder in a conventional sense. But looking at someone I knew, lying in the spot where he breathed his last breath, seeing and smelling the mortification of his body, I couldn't help thinking that this was the result of violence. Looking down from that ledge into a deep pit that once was a West Virginia mountain, I could see every corpse I ever found.

Violence comes in many forms. Yes, Willie stabs Polly in her heart and we know it's a sin—a grave injustice. His guilt is so great, Willie hands himself over to the authorities. We have prisons full of people who are doing hard time for much less. The news keeps us up to date about the latest act of brutality, the newest personal tragedy. But what can we say about the sins of Massey Energy Company who flattens a whole mountain, destroys people's home and poisons their water for profit? We've taken inner-city crime, whether it's the South Bronx or the Westside of Chicago, and made it the face of violence in modern America, but the biggest killers go unpunished. There are some violent acts that will never be prosecuted under the current legal system, whether in the hollows of Appalachia or the streets of Chicago. Greed has murdered more people than any scorned lover or kid with a gun. Poverty is not the sad fate for people who make bad choices; it's the powerful weapon of greed. Poverty is a history of violence upon violence, and all of poverty's manifest suffering may seem senseless and incomprehensible in the same way we never learn what drove Willie to kill Polly. But we've got to see that there's a motive here. Poverty is not a divine mystery. It is a condition human beings have created and have allowed to exist. If we fail to see poverty for what it is, we either will be complicit in the violence or we will be the next victims.

Family cabin on Kayford Mountain, WV
Photo: Quan Blanche, Media Mobilizing Project

Alix Webb
Poverty Initiative

To Be Saved

I began this journey thinking about Dorothea Lange. When I think about white poverty I think of her images—the photos of starving mothers, children and white migrant farm workers, during the Great Depression following work across the South and Appalachia to the West Coast. In the fall of 2006, a new book of Dorothea Lange's photos was released. The book shows works from a period of her life's artwork/photojournalism that had been confiscated and removed from public access by the US government for more than half a century.

During the years of World War II, Lange photographed and documented the incarceration of US citizens of Japanese ancestry in relocation centers and internment/concentration camps here in the US. The 800+ photographs have recently been released and are now available to the public in the national archives. A number of them were taken by Lange in Hayward, California, where my mother's family is from. They are of my family's friends, neighbors, community. My mother was the first baby born at the Merced Relocation Center, in May 1942.

The question on my mind was, what connection is there between the images Lange is most famous for and the ever-so-rare images of my people, my family, my homeland? Was there a simple connection for her? What connection would I find? Appalachia seems very separate from my history as a fourth generation Japanese American here in this country. When visible, the struggle of my people has been portrayed as a struggle of racism and thoroughly embedded in identity-politics.

I came away from this trip with many thoughts about connection. But they are still difficult for me to put into words. Following are a few.

In the US, I was raised Christian (a mix of Episcopalian and Catholic), and I was also raised Japanese-American which, in terms of spirituality, means for me some combination of Buddhist, Shinto, and Japanese culture. A few years ago, I returned to Japan for the first time in twenty years and to Kyoto, Japan's sacred city of ancient temples, ringed by mountains and crisscrossed by streets punctuated by small shrines and statues of figures of worship.

During our trip, a friend arranged for my sister and me to visit a Buddhist garden. It is a very famous garden. The entrance is marked by an enormous ancient stone—a totem—with the garland of rope and white paper lightening that marks the entrance to a sacred space. It is made entirely of moss. When you enter, your footsteps on the path of stones are cushioned in textures of green. The trees and rocks all have mosses like light scarves on their surfaces, like green brushstrokes reflecting yellows, browns, reds and blacks.

For me, being in the garden was a journey through a delicately created sacred landscape. Most Westerners have seen the long scroll paintings (often Chinese) depicting scholars, monks, poets and priests traveling through rocky mountain paths towards high peaks. Some interpret the narrative of these paintings as spiritual journeys towards enlightenment—for the people in the painting and for those who view it. Our eyes can climb (and descend) the painting. There are places to rest. There are treacherous paths. There are spaces and paths where vision is obscured by clouds and rocky barriers. Sometimes one reaches the place to which one journeys. Sometimes one is blocked forever from reaching that place.

This garden for me was the physical experience through such a narrative. We climbed the moss covered stone steps, past tea houses and shrines—our view opening and obscured—towards soft green landscapes, some bare, some lush.

My sister and I took this trip at a time when we knew our grandfather would die here in the US. And our blood-link to the Nisei generation and our heritage would pass. My grandfather was a nursery-man in northern California. And as the post-internment generation, I believe the closest thing my sister and I have felt to a homeland was among his trees, and pots, and earth of his farm, reclaimed and rebuilt after incarceration. During summer visits, my understanding of myself in this country was shaped by the bamboo groves, the almond trees, the rows of bonsai pots, the moon-viewing gate under tall cedar. Since my trip to the garden in Kyoto, the totem rock at the entrance stays in my mind. Some would say it holds a spirit. For me it is an anchor to my history and my ancient and present home.

On a snowy Tuesday afternoon, I rode through the Ridge in Philippi, West Virginia in World Vision's van, guided by Candy and driven by Chris, the coordinators of World Vision's Time-Banking Project. Candy had offered to take us through her home. We drove along a rushing river, whose rocky edges Candy has walked and wandered in summer sun, all her life. We saw large sun-baked stones where she had rested before diving with her friends, family, mother, and sons into the river to ride the current to another stopping point. We wound round and round the mountain ridge on muddy roads, past snowy fields, trailers, small houses, dogs and cattle, and distant hollers and hills. Candy knew who lived in every house, and how they were related to her or other family members. Poverty was visible throughout: in the way family members live in generations of small houses and hand-me-down trailers. In the gas pumps that occupy their yards—placed by oil companies tapping the vast resources of this land for which residents receive a few thousand dollars a year, and all the gas their cars can use. Every few miles Candy would point out a small house, a rough building, some new, some hundreds of years old—all churches lining our route.

After our drive, Chris asked our group about who we were, and we talked about the Poverty Initiative. And we talked about our lives and the Bible. All are the languages of this place and a conversation can only go so far using only one or another. Then we asked them about themselves and the work they do. Candy told us a story about herself—about how she was saved.

It happened in the last year. For some time, Candy had been in a period of deep mourning for the death of her mother. Her mother had died, at Candy's feet, when she came to visit her daughter, a member of the Air Force. Her mother was young, and proud of her daughter. After the death, with little support, Candy had turned to whatever means she could to handle her grief – alcohol, sleep, the words and notes of Tupac. One day, as she was driving to pick up her young sons, she had a vision.

She was home, on the ridge, with all of her family. There was sun, and it was raining gold. And all of her people were there. And they were well.

So vivid, and clear, and simple. So profound. She was saved.

She told us that this is why she came back to the Ridge. She wants that for her people, now. She wants to find how they can have that—the rain of gold, their home, where all are well.

I felt like the connection I had hoped to feel to this region, Appalachia, had begun to form. A connection to a people who have fought so hard in this rough and beautiful landscape. Whose battles are intensely political, whose images are manipulated and misused, whose battle is brilliant, heroic, successful and tragic. Through stories of depression, war, union battles, farms, lives, and deaths. People who have not lost connection to their home. Or their families. Or themselves.

I find that I too have a vision (though still unfolding) of my people—and all people—to live in a land of sun, and plenty, and a rain of gold, and to be whole, and well.

Laurel Creek Church, built in 1901
Chestnut Ridge
Philippi, WV
Photo: Alix Webb

Gayle Irvin

Who Am We?

The journey to Appalachian country was not one journey for me, but several. Sure, I was on the same road with all the others, following the winding, twisting asphalt paths carved out of the hills of West Virginia, Tennessee, and southeastern Ohio, but there were other journeys I was on—all roads traveled before, but new again. What does the song say...everything old is new again.

My journeys have been down well-worn roads in search of identity. The question, prompted by this Appalachian experience...the question that strikes in the darkest nights, is "Who Am I?" More appropriate for my life is the way that Gregg Levoy asks it in his book, *Callings*: "Who am we?" For I am not one person, but many.

I grew up in Joliet, Illinois in the 1950s. At the time it was a deeply segregated town thirty-five miles southwest of Chicago, surrounded by cornfields. I could stick my head out the back seat window of the car as my daddy drove along country roads, close my eyes and breathe deeply the smell of summer. And, it is true that if you go out at night and stand next to a cornfield, you can hear the corn grow. It was also a time when I watched on our old black and white TV as Negroes marched in Selma—little children my age terrorized by German Shepherds and sprayed with fire hoses. I cried, and my daddy looked at the TV and shook his head saying, "This is wrong. Oh, this is not right. Oh, brother me! They're just kids. Come on!" I shook and cried.

When my mother died, it was Mrs. Carter, a black preacher's wife, who came to care for us. Mrs. Carter washed away the blood on the sheets and the floors that had hemorrhaged from my mother's body, and she would come into my room at night when I was sick and couldn't sleep and sing to me. She laid her large beautiful black hand on my skinny belly and sang. I loved Mrs. Carter. And every Christmas, for years, we would get in the car and drive to Mrs. Carter's house on the south side of town. That's when I saw it—the other side of town. Houses so run down and thin, you could see through them. We would deliver a big box of food, cookies and bread. On walking into Mrs. Carter's house, I remember two things. It was the poorest house I had ever been in; and the cleanest. I remember crying on the way home. We didn't have much, but what we had was a mansion compared to the people that lived only a few miles away.

We were a deeply religious family and I took everything I was taught literally. Jesus loved all the little children, red and yellow, black, and white. How could people have such hate? How could we say we we're Christians and at the same time be killing people in cities and towns not far from mine—churches and cars burned, people lynched. If you sided with blacks, would you be killed too?

As the 1960s replaced the 1950s, into our living room came evidence of things changing. The markers of my life became the deaths of John, Bobby, and Martin. When Kennedy was shot, I was scared, and as it grew darker that day, I went into my bedroom, crawled into my closet and cried. Bobby was our new hope, but they killed him too. And they had killed Martin. It seemed all was lost. What was this world I was born into?

By the time the Democratic Convention was held in Chicago, I did not trust anyone or anything in our government and all I wanted was to get out—to get away—away from my home and the people in it.

My grief started to turn to anger and most dinner time conversations turned to the war in Vietnam. My father and I fought bitterly. Most conversation ended with tears, me running away, my father, the WWII vet, not able to conceive of his country in an immoral war.

So, run away I did...no longer the girl I had been brought up to be. No longer religious. No longer patriotic. I was angry and loud. Two days after graduating from high school, I got on a plane headed for Boston, a city swollen with youth, all ready to bring the government down.

It is clear to me now that I had no idea who I was in those days. I just knew what I wasn't. I experimented with everything I could, saved mostly by some reserve sensibility when it came to drugs.

One of my first jobs was as a home health nurse serving people with mental illness. I lived in Maine at the time, and states were closing state psychiatric facilities—the effort known as deinstitutionalization —probably one of those ideas that looks good on paper or certainly helps someone balance a budget somewhere. But the problem is, as it always is in America, there are not enough services to even begin to manage the social problems associated with these initiatives. My "clients" as we called them, were being put into rooming houses and shacks in the towns and country side that were not, in many cases, fit for dogs. I remember visiting one schizophrenic woman in an Augusta, Maine rooming house that backed onto the Kennebec River on Water Street—in the shadow of the capitol building. When I got into her room (a large closet) she sat there with nothing more than a small bag and a blanket, and her hallucinations. It was February, sub-zero outside, and there was no glass in the window. More than once, I argued with the clinic doctor that there would be something wrong with these people if they weren't crazy given the conditions in which they were living! He thought me uncooperative.

It was during this time that I saw some of the worst poverty that exists anywhere. People who lived in ramshackle dwellings, people so poor it was hard to know what kept them alive. But they loved seeing their nurse come. They showed a generosity that was hard to explain. They would want to make me a cup of coffee, which I would try to drink. They had nothing and yet they wanted to offer me something each time I came. Some of the trailers were heated by kerosene and smelled of that and animal feces on the floor. The smoke caused me to come close to vomiting. At one trailer home I always sat by the door and left it ajar; otherwise I could not breathe.

One of my last home health visits before quitting was with a young, mildly retarded woman whose father had signed her out of the hospital against medical advice. We feared he was sexually abusing her. I was told that after driving twenty miles outside of Augusta to take a left on the dirt road and it was the second house on the left. It was the second house on the left—ten miles down a narrow dirt road. When I pulled up to the house, two dogs ran towards the car, barking right into the drivers window, teeth bared. The girl's father came out of the house with a shot gun. It took the better part of twenty minutes to get him to allow me to get out of the car and enter the house. It took another thirty for me to convince him to let me go upstairs and meet with his daughter. They were as poor as dirt.

I left nursing because, despite the fact that I felt I was doing worthy work, I was making $6 an hour, a dollar more than bag-boys in the local grocery store. I had two girls of my own now and wanted more for them.

So, I went to work in a corporation, starting out at entry level and working my way up, going to college and earning a degree. It took me eight years working full time, but I graduated with honors. I read *Dress for Success*, wore my hair up, and bought a navy blue suit and high heels. One thing led to another, and twenty-five years later, I was working for a Fortune 500 company in New York City and making more money than anyone in my family ever had.

There's more to the story, for sure, but I'm going to skip all that for now, and just say that a year ago, I left corporate America. I gave all kinds of reasons, but the primary one was that I felt dead in my soul. And now I'm in Appalachia, a land that feels more home to me than anywhere I have been in years. My daddy's dead. We barely reconciled once, but I became a person he just couldn't know. At a recent funeral, my cousins were looking at me and saying—you were the rebel. You were the one that got away. The fact is, I don't know what I got away from—the possibility of a very limited life for sure. But who am I, and where is home? I'm more at home in a subway car in New York City or in a holler in Appalachia then I am anywhere else. Where I'm not at home anymore is in the boardrooms of the world, or the bland hotel conference rooms where I frequently find myself. Oh, I can talk-the-talk. I know all the business buzz words and can throw them around like a juggler at the fair. But you can't stand on the ridge of a Tennessee Mountain overlooking the devastation of strip-mining and corporate greed and not be moved. If you are not, then you are dead.

Greed is what drives much of what goes on in corporations. Trust me on this. But then, knowing what I know, I can't just blame the corporations. I am the corporation. What lives in the corporation, lives in me. It lives in all of us.

My journey to Appalachia was a spiritual, cultural and social journey. And it took me down my well-worn road of identity. That question—the one that strikes in the darkness of night, the cold steel at your back —is the question, "Who Am I?"

~~~~~~~~~~~~~~~~~~~~

I'm on a train right now, heading straight for our nation's capitol. I look from my comfortable seat out the window and see apartment buildings near collapse, broken down neighborhoods, wretchedness and poverty everywhere I look. Is this where my work is? Or is my work with the very organizations that are causing this great inequity in our land?

When I worked among the most poor and oppressed in this great land of ours, the work felt real. I could feel what I was doing; I was in touch with who I was.

Somehow or other, going to Appalachia was a coming home to myself, a self that I left before. A friend of mine suggested that I'm in a really good position to have a foot in both worlds—that I am a "bridger," she said—a translator. Well maybe, but I foresee many a sleepless night before I resolve this one. And maybe it never gets resolved.

I've learned and told others that in order to become the person we truly want to be, we must be absolutely who we are, in all its fullest, integrating all the parts of ourselves, and that includes, as Zorba the Greek would say, "The Whole Catastrophe."
~~~~~~~~~~~~~~~~~~~~

Paul Chapman
Poverty Initiative

Should I Move to Appalachia?

> *Con los pobres de la tierra quiero yo mi suerte echar.*
> (With the poor people of the earth I want to cast my lot.)

All my adult life I've heard this song, "Guantanamera," as a call that has haunted me. It echoes in the biblical word that the presence of God will be found among the least of our brothers and sisters.

When on Wednesday in Charleston, the Rev. Matthew Watts asked if we were called to live in West Virginia, I heard the echo once again.

To follow Jesus is to live with the poor, to enter so deeply into the community of poor people that one can know what Jesus knew when he said, "Blessed are the poor." To this end, I meditate on the so-called "Nazareth years," when Jesus lived in apparent obscurity, presumably as a carpenter among a people where craftsmen were very low on the socio-economic pyramid, somewhere between peasant and outcast. What does this say to one who wishes to follow Jesus?

The pastoral letter of the Appalachian Catholic bishops, "This Land is Home to Me,"[1] written over thirty years ago, still rings true. To live with the poor is to live with God's special people.

> They sing of a life
> free and simple,
> with time for one another,
> and for peoples needs,
> based on the dignity of the human person,
> at one with nature's beauty,
> crowned by poetry.

I believe that the true spirit of America is best known, not in the glitz, but in the integrity of those whom the world sees last and counts least. In another place the bishops write:

[1] www.osjspm.org/majordoc_this_is_home_to_me.aspx

> Once we all
> • knew how to dance and sing
> • sat in mystery before the poets' spell
> • felt our hearts rise to nature's cathedral.
> Now an alien culture
> battles to shape us
> into plastic forms empty of Spirit,
> into beasts of burden
> without mystery.

How would I live here among the poor? I would not come with answers to their many "problems." I would come to listen and learn.

> We must
> continually take time and invest creativity
> into listening to the people,
> especially the poor.
> For it is they who,
> out of their frustrations, dreams and struggles,
> must lead the way for all of us.

And again

> If a new society is to be born,
> it will emerge from the grass roots.

Living here, I would not want to be economically dependent on my neighbors, for while generosity is everywhere here, in many places there is simply no economic foundation on which to survive.

Let us not romanticize the life of the poor. This is a very harsh life. Would I have the stamina?

To be one with the local people would require time – time to discard some of the power values that separate me from the poorest and to become one with those who, in his time, nurtured Jesus.

> For it is the weak things of this world
> which seem like folly,
> that the Spirit takes up
> and makes its own.
> The dream of the mountain's struggle,
> the dream of simplicity
> and of justice,
> like so many other repressed visions
> is, we believe,
> the voice of Yahweh among us.

Could there possibly be a more noble life calling?

Anne King
Columbia University School of Social Work

Growing Pains

Our trip to Appalachia calls to my mind William Blake's two books of poetry, *Songs of Innocence* and *Songs of Experience*. The former speaks of a child's view of the world: verdant, rolling hills, a giving world filled with love and happiness. As age begins to rear its head, these hills lose their luster and the light of innocence fades. "Mercy has a human heart" swiftly evolves into "Cruelty has a human heart." Blake might say that I lost my childhood in Appalachia.

My awareness of poverty previously came from the pages of books, magazines, the images presented to me through television and photographs. All of which kept the reality of poverty at bay. It frightens me that the media is effectively the conveyor of "truth." There are people all over the country—all over the world—whose eyes and ears are filled with mere interpretations of an impoverished lifestyle. In these stories, every poverty-stricken face just becomes another face.

I know I bought it, particularly growing up in an affluent bubble in Oklahoma City. Neither I, nor any other innocent soul, can be faulted for such gullibility. We are shielded from reality by the boundaries so well maintained by our society. Homeless shelters exist on islands nearly inaccessible to residents. Earth irreparably destroyed can only be seen by driving miles up a dirt road off of the freeway, where mountains still appear to undauntedly tower over the passing cars. Ramshackle homes, with peeling paint, caved-in roofs, and crooked frames, also hide on roads rarely traveled by anyone other than those forced to call this home. I must admit, not having to see real poverty provided me with a level of comfort that I no longer feel. How can I be comfortable hearing the whole truth from those who live the experience?

Times are hard in Appalachia. In many ways, they are getting harder as coal companies increase their efforts to satiate their greed. Yet, it's not hopeless. The ties that bind are incredibly strong in the region. Much of this can be attributed to the culture of religion and its unifying force. The integrity of community members must take credit for the rest. People like Candy Adams with World Vision in Philippi, WV; Professor Rich Greenlee of Ohio State University; Evelyn Dortch with Direct Action Welfare Group (DAWG) in Charleston, WV and Larry Gibson with the Stanley Heirs Foundation at Mt. Kayford in West Virginia are only a few we encountered on our journey who manifest the qualities of leadership and feel pulled to make their voices heard. Appalachia is absolutely filled with people who believe in their own power to make the structural changes necessary to end their suffering. We had the opportunity to listen to life stories in a more tangible way than can be recreated in any media, certainly not in these words I write here.

The people of Appalachia have inspired me to do what I can to ensure that their much-concealed hardship continues to be revealed through their own committed mouths. Despite the knowledge that one human can have such disregard for the well-being of another, I'm eager to turn my new-found "experience" from anger into productive action, just as those who live it have done. The innocent eyes of a child do not have to be the only eyes that see the mercy of humankind.

Two weeks after returning from Appalachia immersion participants gathered for further reflection. In the final exercise we each shared the ways in which we will respond to what we learned, using yarn to weave our commitments together. Led in song by Charon Hribar (right) are (left to right) Peter Cava, Paul Chapman, Anne King, Katy Moore, Judith Scott, Jessica Chadwick, and Alix Webb.
Upper Refectory, Union Theological Seminary
Photo: Colleen Wessel-McCoy

Highlander Research and Education Center
New Market, TN
Photo: Sara Smith, Media Mobilizing Project

Megan Lloyd Joiner
Union Theological Seminary

The Appalachia That I Know

The Appalachia that I know is the stuff of dreams. The crystal clear waters of my childhood, so cold they take your breath away became the balm of my adolescence and sooth me to this day. But it is in my nightmares that the dirt road down which I traveled every summer has been paved, hi-rises built where sunflowers once strained toward the mid-day over-the-mountain sun, a bustling town has taken the place of the Quaker community that I have known and loved nestled there in those mountains filled with tobacco farms and rhododendron. I walk along the familiar forest path into unknown territory. Capitalism has come to my safe haven; my friends have given up and traded the garden that was once my pride and joy for hot dog stands and cotton candy vendors.

After one of these dreams I wake with tears and sweat and have to remind myself (it always takes a while) that they are still there, the children I knew now grown. The campers I cradled during their own nightmares have become the life-guards at the river, the cooks in the kitchen. The magic of our mountain home lives on.

The mountains of this western North Carolina county were mined, not for coal, but for mica. Each summer a popular activity was a trip to the mica mine on the other end of the county to see the sparkly translucent mineral in its mined form. Mica was once used as window panes in cabins and houses throughout the mountains. Now it is found in cosmetics and plastics. I never went to the mine. Mica sparkles in the soil, in the sand by the river, in the rocks I could see through the waters. The ground literally shown at night, guiding my bare feet along the well-worn path to where I could crawl into the branches of the mighty trees planted there by the water, unmoving, solid, safe. The water so frigid because it came straight from the mountain. The river was alive, continually moving, but ever constant. I was baptized there in that water without knowing it. It gave me life and continues to even now here in this city—by another river—as I hear the stories of my friends, classmates and colleagues who have returned from the mountains.

They have known the dreams and the nightmares. They have stood on the mountain tops and seen my fears come true. We all have a haven—a holler—for some of us it is in these Appalachian mountains, loved by generations of diverse peoples, stolen many times over. Until we understand that it is the beauty of the land itself that sparkles, that it is not ours to take, unlimited, never to be restored, that we are guests here in a land that bestows upon us safety, comfort, and life itself, we will continue to wake up sweaty and crying, the loss of our mountains a reality. To do so, we must know each other's stories. We must cross the lines of culture and class, race and gender—lines often especially strong in the mountains. We must cross these lines to learn that we all love this land, and that the land has become a part of us. When we know this, we will understand that we are a part of each other. For it is only together that we will save each other and our mountains.

Lee Gregg
Multicultural Genealogical Center
Chesterhill, OH
Photo: Sarah Smith, Media Mobilizing Project

Mildred T. Vore
Multicultural Genealogical Center
Chesterhill, Ohio
Photo: Sarah Smith, Media Mobilizing Project

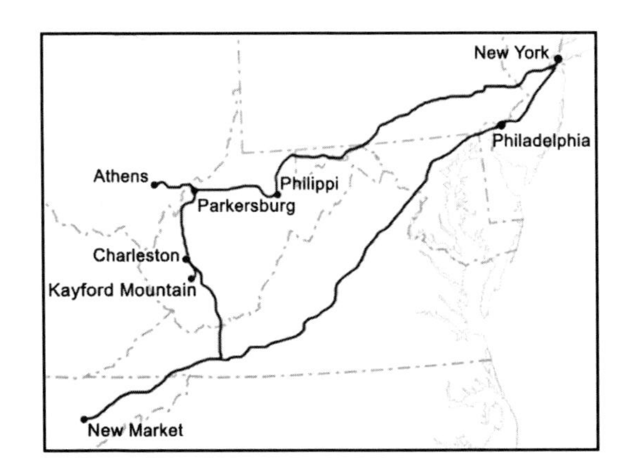

Biblical Reflection

Chapter 13

Selene Kaye reading Ruth
Highlander Research and
Education Center
New Market, TN
Photo: Colleen Wessel-McCoy

Erin Flemming
Union Theological Seminary

Reading Ruth in Appalachia

Nearly every day during the Poverty Initiative Immersion Course in Appalachia, the students engaged in an hour of textual reflection, which I had the opportunity to lead. While we referenced various modern secular texts on social justice and Appalachia, the main text throughout the week was the biblical book of Ruth, the story of the widowed Moabite woman who chooses to leave her homeland and journey to Bethlehem in Judah with her mother-in-law Naomi, and who eventually becomes the great-grandmother of King David. After much brainstorming with many different people, I chose Ruth not only because I love the story but also because I suddenly saw so many connections between this book and the region of Appalachia. The rural setting, the importance of land and kinship, the difficulties surrounding outsiders and the immense poverty of the story resonated with what I knew about the region. The book of Ruth also contains several journeys, which mean different things for different characters. I thought it was appropriate since the participants of the immersion course were on a journey together, with nearly 50 different people from various backgrounds and perspectives. However, I discovered when we began the trip that journeys have also comprised a major part of people's lives in Appalachia for nearly a century. People often have to move out of the region to find work, but many eventually "come back home" for good.

As I did research to learn more about Ruth, I noticed that, while scholars mention the poverty of Ruth and Naomi in passing, I had difficulty finding a commentary that explicitly focused on the issue of poverty. This surprised me since it is one of few biblical narratives in which the protagonists are destitute. In contrast, Ruth is also one of few biblical books that features women as its main characters, and there has been plenty of ink spilled over gender relations in the story.

Throughout the incredibly enlightening discussions we had as a group, four major themes emerged surrounding the book of Ruth and our experiences in Appalachia:

"Deserving" versus "Undeserving" Poor: Throughout the book of Ruth, Ruth is described as a "worthy" woman. Boaz, a prominent man of Bethlehem, recognizes her worth and provides extra food for Ruth and Naomi and protection for Ruth as she works. He eventually marries Ruth, and she becomes a recognized part of the Israelite community. During the trip, we discussed images of poverty and questioned the designations of who should "deserve" help and who should not. Charity organizations usually promote images of people who seem innocent and helpless, particularly children. I noticed that the literature of World Vision, an organization that is dedicated to relief work for the counties surrounding Philippi, West Virginia only showed pictures of children or volunteers. By contrast, Professor Tom Horacek who spoke to us on January 9, does much of his research in a women's prison. He discussed the importance of looking at the poverty statistics of prisoners—statistics that are not usually considered. Incarcerated persons, not typically depicted as the "deserving" poor, are also often victims of structural poverty, which is a major contributing factor in their participation in illegal activities.

Hospitality: In the second chapter of the book, Ruth takes the initiative to glean in the fields during the barley harvest to provide food for herself and her mother-in-law. In doing so, she takes advantage of Israelite law, which required farmers to leave a part of their harvest for the poor, the alien, and the widow to glean (Lev 19:9-10; 23:22; Deut 24:19-22). When Boaz learns that Ruth is gleaning in his field, he tells her to glean only from his field during the harvest. Boaz's actions towards her are examples of hospitality protocol: providing protection and legal identity for Ruth during harvest. Moreover, Boaz invites Ruth to the midday meal and offers her bread and wine. By inviting her to a meal, Boaz effectively makes Ruth part of his household and gives her special gleaning privileges. Throughout the immersion course, we were given food, rest, warmth, and community. The various organizations we met went out of their way to provide for us and gave their time and energy to educate us about their models of ending poverty in Appalachia.

Social structures that provide for the poor/structures that keep people in poverty: Certainly in Ruth's story, the Israelite law that allowed the poor, the alien, and the widow to glean at harvest time is a legal structure that provides for the disadvantaged members of a society. Moreover, Ruth and Naomi rely on Boaz as Naomi's kinsman to redeem their property and provide for them. Although most biblical scholars do not think that this matches actual social practices in ancient Israel, the story rotates around the principle that kinship groups have a responsibility to provide for each other. However, a major topic of discussion during our textual reflections was the social structures, reflected in Ruth, which kept women in poverty if their husbands died. At the beginning of the story, Naomi sees her worth in terms of reproduction, because having children was women's primary contribution to society. Past childbearing age and without sons, she declares on her return to Bethlehem that "the Lord has brought [her] back empty" despite the fact that Ruth is with her. It is one thing to identify these problematic structures in the short story of Ruth but much more difficult to point them out and change these structures in the world around us. Currently, our government's structures that are intended to provide for the poor play a part in keeping people in poverty. Identifying and breaking the social structures that perpetuate poverty is at the heart of the Poverty Initiative's mission.

Individual identity within a community: The book of Ruth is set during a time when people's identities were determined by gender, birth order, birthplace, tribe, and nationality. Many biblical scholars think that Ruth was probably written as a counter-text to the injunctions to divorce foreign wives found in Ezra-Nehemiah by showing a righteous foreign woman who assimilated into Judean society and became the ancestress to the most lauded king in Israel's history. Identity and community repeatedly came up during the immersion course, and we talked a lot with folks about their identities as Appalachians and also the negative stereotypes that surround this identity.

Sign in front of a church in Chestnut Ridge
Philippi, WV
Photo: Alix Webb

Kim Tomaszewski
Union Theological Seminary

Excerpts from a Sermon on Appalachia

Only a few weeks ago I spent ten days in the region known as Appalachia—mostly in West Virginia, then in eastern parts of Ohio, and finally in Tennessee. Prior to the Twentieth Century the people of Appalachia were geographically isolated from the rest of the country because of the surrounding mountains. They were stopped in time, and now are subjected to years of progress that occurred throughout the rest of the country, just over the mountains...just incommunicable to them.

In the Eighteenth Century the first commercial coal mines in the United States were started in 1748, in Midlothian Virginia, near Richmond, bringing the big city's interests to Appalachia. And with this, the lives of these small farmers and countrymen were quickly changed.

The coal industry employed over 175,000 men throughout Appalachia. Coal mining became just as much a part of the culture as the music and foods. Black lung struck down young fathers, and young sons took their place in the mines as the bread winners. At least, coal mining provided jobs for the already working-poor, jobs which were much needed in these small mountain towns.

By the 1880s, coal-cutting machines became available with the Nineteenth Century's industrialization. But today, the modern approach to mining, mountaintop removal, or "peak reduction," as the coal companies call it, has dramatically cut the number of employees from hundreds of thousands to, in some mines, forty-five, none of which are from the Appalachia region.

Mountain Top Removal allows the coal companies to remove as much as 700 feet from a mountain, using explosives in order to get at the coal below. In Larry Gibson's words, "They used to take the coal from the mountain. Now they take the mountain from the coal." It will take 3,000 years for the ecosystem to restore itself when the mining is done. 3,000 years. A long time. ... But the mountains are gone forever.

The 900 acres surrounding Larry Gibson's family's 50-acre plot on Kayford Mountain in Boone County, West Virginia are owned by the Massey Energy Company, the fifth largest coal company in the United States. His great,

great-grandfather settled on Kayford Mountain 186 years ago and more than 300 of his relatives are buried there. For the last twenty years though, Larry's memories, traditions and family safety have been threatened by the encroaching coal industry. The Massey Energy Company wants his land and they have no qualms about pushing him off of it, regardless of the history and roots he may have in it. A colleague of mine reflected, "[Larry's] trailer has been vandalized, shot at and flipped over. His dogs have been killed. His truck was pushed into a river. The area around his home is periodically showered with debris from the explosions at the nearby mine. Sink holes have developed in the family cemetery and carried off the remains of many of his loved ones." And if these things weren't enough, he is reminded each day by the inescapable noises of the heavy machinery that persist in destroying the mountains around him.

We walked together, with Larry, only eight hundred yards from his front door where this was taking place. Where the Appalachia Mountains once stood majestically, protectively, and nourishingly, there is a wound in the land. And as we watched, it continued to be abused. It is happening even now. And once again, in the words of my friend who witnessed this with me, who was supported by supporting me after watching this, "It will happen until there is nothing left and then it will happen elsewhere".

Larry said to us, "If you're not going to do something about this, you're wasting my time!" And then when we sang and cried together he said, "You folks...you really are going to do something, aren't you?"

During our time in Appalachia a local priest read to us from his New Revised Standard Version (NRSV) of the Bible. He read Psalm 11:3, "If the foundations are crumbling what will the righteous do?" This line really struck me and so I went to my pocket New International Version (NIV) to underline it. However, my translation read, "When the foundations are being destroyed, what can the righteous do?"

The same passage in the Hebrew Bible, the Old Testament, but when the two translations are compared with one another, they illustrate two very different messages:

> "If the foundations are crumbling, what will the righteous do?"
>
> "When the foundations are being destroyed, what can the righteous do?"

When thinking about the themes of Ruth that we studied and the relationship between these and coal miners in Appalachia, and with the poor in general, we must understand the notion of having (or not having) choice. Ruth is dependent on Boaz for the survival of the next generation, for her well-being, as well as for her mother-in-law's. People who work in manual labor are thought of as expendable but they must work in the coal mines—dying early and cruelly, working in terrible conditions, forced from education into labor, and often times bringing their family into this line of work to face the same—just in order to support their family; in order to survive. What is the difference in hearing "What can you do" and "What will you do"?

What does this say about responsibility? About one's capabilities? About one's willingness? When we ask ourselves "What will we do?" we begin to live our traditions of interconnectedness. We begin to ask to take responsibility for one another.

We, the member congregations of the Unitarian Universalist Association, covenant to affirm and promote

- *The inherent worth and dignity of every person;*
- *Justice, equity and compassion in human relations;*
- *The goal of world community with peace, liberty and justice for all;*
- *Respect for the interdependent web of all existence of which we are a part.*

Four of our seven principles speak directly to our relationship with one another, asking us to take responsibility for the world.

In working with the Poverty Initiative, we often go back to the Biblical quotation "The poor will be with you always." We do not take this for granted, but ask continually, "What can we do?".

One last note on this: It was said to us at one point on the trip, "It is a privilege to be able to choose the injustice you want to fight." Choice. Who among us really has the privilege of choice?

Larry Gibson and the many thousands like him around the world, like our heroin Ruth—the impoverished and oppressed—are our hope; not because they are kings or patriarchs, but because they are the poor, they are the survivors, and because they do not ask, "What can we do?" Instead, they have no choice but to act. If we do not stand up and choose to fight injustices, what are we choosing but to empower those who are creating the problem? If we are to be of any use on this earth we must make their struggle our own.

There is so much more to tell from my experience during those ten days in Appalachia. But more than anything, I have wondered whose translation I am reading? And also, at what point does one get angry enough, sad enough and aware enough to also be one who acts without choice? It does not have to be just the poor who are faced with these decisions. I ask that we all take the responsibility to uphold our traditions, like Ruth, who stayed with her mother-in-law, subjecting herself to being the security of another.

Final Thoughts

Chapter 14

Quan Blanche, member of Media Mobilizing Project, filming at the Multicultural Genealogical Center
Chesterhill, OH
Photo: Erica Almiron, Media Mobilizing Project

Phil Wider
Media Mobilizing Project

The Media Mobilizing Project

Why this trip?

The Media Mobilizing Project (MMP) participated in the Appalachia Immersion in order to deepen and develop relationships, both within our group and between us and members of the Poverty Initiative. The trip also gave us an opportunity to forge personal relationships with the Appalachian people who hosted, inspired and informed us.

As members of the MMP, it's essential to place the work we do in Philadelphia and Pennsylvania in its bigger context—both nationally and globally, as well as historically. By exposing us to the specifics of another concrete place—both historically and presently, the trip to Appalachia provided just such an opportunity. For example, as a group that works with poverty in a big city like Philadelphia, it was incredibly valuable for the MMP to acquaint ourselves with the particularities of poverty in Appalachia. Similarly, the Poverty Initiative's attention to the building of a movement to end poverty, led by the interests of those most affected by poverty, provides an important historical context for our work.

Through developing these relationships and expanding our awareness and consciousness, the trip prepared us to take up our work back home more strategically and effectively.

On Media

As a group that works with media as a tool for organizing and movement building, we came into this trip particularly sensitive to the voices and reality of poor people—a growing segment of our society—that is rarely heard and often obscured. While we know this to be true in Philadelphia, we also found this to be the case in Appalachia throughout its history. While I had known that coal mines had stolen the wealth of the region, I had not been aware of how the media had stolen something perhaps even more devastating—the region's voice and identity. Any movement for equality and justice will have to once again give expression to that voice and identity. For me, a group like the Direct Action Welfare Group (DAWG) of Charleston best represents that prospect. They have known the burden of poverty in their daily lives and they intend to change that for their children and the generation to come.

On Singing

During our trip I was particularly impressed by the importance of song. After particularly tense theological reflections, where people were struggling to find each other, song was useful in bringing us together. After a day of appreciating complexity, song was useful for simplifying things. After experiencing the devastation of mountain top removal and the harshness of a failing economic system on people's lives, song lifted us and focused us on the work that lies ahead.

At various low moments in the course of the trip, songs sung in a heartfelt way were powerful instruments that sustained and cohered our group. In the face of harsh realities and in the midst of long days and nights struggling with one another to understand the reality we were experiencing, time and time again we could turn to song.

While we sang songs birthed in the civil rights movement and union struggles of previous days, we also added new verses, giving meaning in our contemporary context. The harmony of our voices singing different parts sounded beautiful and helped hold out the possibility that what we were trying to do is possible.

Conclusion

We were a powerful combination of seminary students, social workers, media organizers and arts and cultural workers, each group having a critical role in a movement to end poverty and human misery.

As a Jew, I never thought I'd go through Appalachia with a group of Christian seminary students, and I never thought that I'd hope a friend of mine would become a Christian minister. But the trip clarified for me how important religion is in the majority of people's lives in this country, and it's incredibly important for the Union students I traveled with to become religious leaders dedicated to building a movement to end poverty.

John Wessel-McCoy and Derrick McQueen lead everyone in song.
Philippi Baptist Church basement
Philippi, WV
Photo: Colleen Wessel-McCoy

Coal chute near Kayford Mountain
Photo: Erica Almiron, Media Mobilizing Project

PAUL CHAPMAN
Poverty Initiative

Epilogue

The assigned preparatory reading for the Immersion course included several articles protesting the stereotyping of the residents of Appalachia, by pigeonholing Appalachians as "hillbillies" with their quaint customs, their moonshine history and their distinctive music. Applying these characterizations, we paint mental pictures of unique people who are part of the diverse fabric that we celebrate—essential to what's special about America, and we tend to normalize their poverty as part of that special culture, forgetting that poverty diminishes life.

I hoped that on our trip we would pierce through the stereotypes and see Appalachians in a different light, no longer accepting the conventional wisdom. While honoring the unique culture and vitality of the Appalachian people, I have seen a people who are on the edge of survival—people who have been exploited by the timber and coal industries, and by-passed by technical changes that benefited other segments of the population. The stereotyping helps to obscure some of the daily-life reality of the men and women who are victims of structural neglect and poverty—victims of an economy of greed.

Often in our travels I was reminded of last year's Immersion course to the Gulf Coast. In Florida, Mississippi and Louisiana, participants witnessed not just the results of the hurricanes, but the failure of government to provide for the general welfare, just as we have in Appalachia. Rather than address the root causes of poverty, our business-friendly government has ignored the consequences of an economy that has devastated the land and neglected the people. In the epilogue of the book from the 2006 Immersion course, *Katrina: Listening With Our Hearts*, I wrote "It is increasingly clear that the tragedy of Katrina was an inevitable consequence of an economic system that diminishes human life. It is an economic system that has developed in the west over hundreds of years and that puts profits and economic expansion before the welfare of it citizens. It is a system of individualism in which everyone is supposed to be personally responsible for their own destiny, and dedication to the common good is devalued."

I realize that as a beneficiary of the resources so cruelly extracted form the earth of West Virginia and beyond that I am complicit in the very evil I condemn. And while I am disenchanted with the evil I deplore, I both actively and passively, participate in it, even while realizing the human damage that our system inflicts on its citizens.

Again quoting from *Katrina: Listening with Our Hearts*, "In faith we hold on to a vision of a just world in which everyone will be fulfilled. We believe that the world was created for goodness and that Jesus was able to live free of the life-destroying forces that surrounded him, always dedicated to a world of abundance for all people."

Community mural celebrating local heroes
Along St. Rt. 13 in downtown Glouster, OH
Photo: Colleen Wessel-McCoy

Katrina: Listening With Our Hearts

In January, 2006, a Poverty Initiative Immersion Course took students to the Gulf Coast where participants witnessed not just the tragic results of the hurricanes, but the failure of the government to provide for the general welfare and an "abysmal betrayal of human solidarity." The book we wrote following that trip, *Katrina: Listening With Our Hearts,* states that hurricanes Katrina, Rita and Wilma exposed the awful truth that the curse of poverty affects every section of this country, that poverty in Mississippi, Alabama and Louisiana are but a microcosm of the whole.

If you want to order *Katrina: Listening With Our Hearts,* please get in touch with us.

Poverty Initiative at Union
Theological Seminary
poverty@uts.columbia.edu
3041 Broadway
New York, NY 10027
212-280-1439
www.povertyinitiative.org

Media Mobilizing Project members (left to right—front) Mariko Franz, Desi Burnette, (middle) Sarah Smith, Erika Almiron, Shivaani Selvaraj, Nijme Dzuriko, Phil Wider, (back) Mica Root, Quan Blanche, and Aaron Couch.
Philippi, WV
Photo: unknown

COURSE PARTICIPANTS

CUSSW—Columbia University School of Social Work; MMP—Media Mobilizing Project; UTS—Union Theological Seminary

Erika Almiron, MMP

Willie Baptist, PI

Adam Barnes, UTS

Quan Blanche, MMP

Odis Braxton, UTS

Desi Burnette, MMP

Chris Caruso

Peter Cava, UTS

Jessica Chadwick, UTS & CUSSW

Paul Chapman, PI

Ben Cherland, UTS

Lovelle Clark, UTS

Ellie Martin Cliffe, UTS

Aaron Couch, MMP

Nijme Dzurinko, MMP

Erin Fleming, UTS

Mariko Franz, MMP

Eva Gordon, CUSSW

Chris Grove

Charon Hribar, UTS

Gayle Irvin

Kumiko Kawasaki, CUSSW

Selene Kaye, CUSSW

Dorothy Keith

Anne King, CUSSW

Derrick McQueen, UTS

Katy Moore, UTS

Drew Paton, UTS

Jessica Pulido, CUSSW

Jan Rehmann, UTS

Mica Root, MMP

Andrea Roske-Metcalfe, UTS

Ben Sanders, UTS

Stefanie Schoen, UTS

Tallu Schuyler, UTS

Judith Scott, UTS

Shivaani Selvaraj, MMP

Jason Seymour, UTS

Sarah Smith, MMP

Joe Strife, UTS

Sara Suman, CUSSW

Liz Theoharis, UTS

Paul Thorson, UTS

Kim Tomaszewski, UTS

Justin Ward, UTS

Alix Webb, PI

Colleen Wessel-McCoy, UTS

John Wessel-McCoy

Phil Wider, MMP

In addition, the following people participated in the Orientation but did not travel with the group.

Megan Lloyd Joiner, UTS

Raymond Thomas

Todd Wolfson

Alix Webb
Photo: Sarah Smith, Media Mobilizing Project

Aknowledgements

We acknowledge with gratitude the people who welcomed us into their communities and taught us so much.

Candy Adams
Ada Woodson Adams
Te Bernard
Cheryl Blosser
Larry Bresler
William Burnett
Vilbert Cambridge
Gaston Caperton
Marvin Carr
Sarah Carr
William Carroll
Candy Carawan
Guy Carawan
Robert Daugherty
Lillian Dinos
Evelyn Dortch
Carol Duffield
Doug Duffield
Suzie Francis
Danny Franke
Jack Frech
Kay Gallagher
Bob Garbo
Larry Gibson
Darreen Gray
Rich Greenlee
Jan Griesinger
Marty Hamilton
Jerry Hartley
Samuel Hickman
Tom Horacek
Beth Howard
Mary Howell
Gina Jeremiah
Deanda Johnson
Nancy Keller
Bill Klaus
Ann Kramer
Bruce Kuhre
Stephen Markwood
Julian Martin
Bob McConnell
Peg McDargh
Dennis McNaboe
Chris Miller
Tim Moyers
Chris Mullett
Jane Forrest Redfern
Jessie Roberson
Roberta Roberson
Amy Robison
Owen Rogers
Susan Sarnoff
Bernard Schmitt
Donna Seaman
Ruston Seaman
Janelle Skinner
Dennis Sparks
Mary Steinmaus
Dick Stevens
Dennis Stull
Mary Ann Sympson
Christie Truly
Mildred Vore
Keith Wasserman
Matthew Watts
Jeanne Wells
Lois Whealey
John Winnenberg
Susan Williams
Ana Woodson Wilson
Allen Withers
Sharron Witherspoon
Patricia Wray
Evan Young

We acknowledge with gratitude the organizations who hosted us and shared generously with us.

African American Research and Service Institute, Ohio University, Athens

Alderson-Broaddus College, Philippi, WV

Appalachian People's Action Coalition, Plains, OH

Appalachian Scholar's Program, Ohio University, Athens

Athens County Jobs and Family Services, Chauncey, OH

Columbia University School of Social Work, New York, NY

Department of Social Work, Ohio University, Athens

Direct Action Welfare Group, Charleston, WV

Episcopal Church of the Good Shepherd, Athens, OH

First Presbyterian Church, Athens, OH

Good Works, Inc., Athens, OH

South Parkersburg Baptist Church, Parkersburg, WV

Head Start, Philippi, WV

Highlander Research and Education Center, New Market, TN

Little Cities of Black Diamonds, Shawnee, OH

Media Mobilizing Project, Philadelphia, PA

Monday Creek Restoration Project, New Straitsville, OH

Multicultural Genealogical Center, Chesterhill, OH

National Association of Social Workers, West Virginia Chapter, Charleston, WV

New Straitsville Local History Group, New Straitsville, OH

Organize! Ohio, Athens, OH

People's Chapel, Chestnut Ridge, Philippi, WV

Philippi Baptist Church, Philippi, WV

Picture the Homeless, Bronx, NY

Rendville Art Works, Rendville OH

Rural Action, Trimble, OH

Pope John XXIII Pastoral Center, Charleston, WV

Southern Perry County Youth Arts and Media Initiative (SPiCYAM), Shawnee, OH

Tri-county Community Action, Logan, OH

The Employment Project, New York, NY

Union Theological Seminary, New York, NY

United Campus Ministries Center for Spiritual Growth and Social Justice, Athens, OH

Upshur Cooperative Parish, Buckhannon, WV

Volunteers of America, New York, NY

West Virginia Council of Churches, Charleston

West Virginia Department of Health and Human Resources, Charleston

West Virginia Workforce Investment Council, Charleston

World Vision Appalachia, Philippi, WV

The Poverty Initiative wishes to thank the many people and organizations who helped to make this trip possible. Especially we acknowledge with gratitude the following:

American Baptist Churches / USA Domestic Development Grant

Metzger Price Fund

Samuel Rubin Foundation

Van Riper / Ellis Broadway Baptist Church of Fair Lawn, New Jersey

Geoff and Ginger Worden

More people than we could possibly list here have helped create the vision for and the reality of the Poverty Initiative. We are truly grateful.

Approaching the Gates of Hell
Kayford Mountain, WV
Photo: Alix Webb